Education
in Britain
since 1944

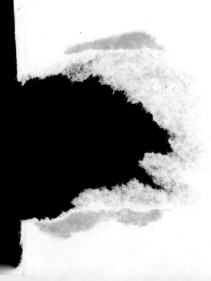

Education
in Britain
since 1944

A personal retrospect

W Kenneth Richmond

Methuen & Co Ltd

First published in 1978 by Methuen and Co Ltd
11 New Fetter Lane, London EC4P 4EE
Printed in Great Britain at the
University Press, Cambridge
Typeset by Red Lion Setters, Holborn, London

ISBN 0 416 85760 4 (hardbound)
ISBN 0 416 85940 2 (paperback)

Contents

1 An age of discontinuity

You have never heard of *Merulius lachrymans?* Unless you happen to be a surveyor, a carpenter or a mycologist it is highly unlikely that you will be acquainted with the species. Unseen, insidiously, it spreads its microscopic spores through woodwork and plaster, feeding on moisture as it grows, until one day floorboards collapse, a staircase caves in and all at once the unfortunate householder finds himself faced with a massive repair bill. Too late, he discovers to his cost that *Merulius lachrymans* is well and truly named.

To begin by suggesting that British education is currently in a near-ruinous state is bound to seem less than convincing and to diagnose it as a case of advanced dry rot may be thought a pun in poor taste. Outwardly, at least, its structure has every appearance of being sound and in good working order. Still, appearances can be deceptive and there are good reasons for suspecting that there is something rotten in the present state of affairs: how else to explain the growing public concern about falling standards and the widespread talk about an alleged decline in the quality of life? Lord Hailsham, for one, is inclined to believe that the Constitution itself, time-honoured and unwritten as it is, is no longer weatherproof nor its foundations secure. In fields other than education abrupt discontinuities in the politics of planning are the order of the day. In terms of René Thom's catastrophe theory, in short, we find ourselves in a situation in which the lines of force are so conflicting that the only certainty is that whatever happens next will be dramatically unlike what has gone before.

In any case it is as well to begin by acknowledging that education is no longer 'in'. Such an acknowledgment has to be made quite independently of the depressed state of Britain's economic affairs and the low morale which accompanies it. In the U.S.A., Sweden and West Germany — countries still enjoying an affluence which we can only envy — leading thinkers share this same sense of disenchantment with the established system of education. Throughout the Western World, indeed, the mood of buoyant optimism which characterized the 1950s and 60s, the years of expansion, has been replaced by one of profound scepticism, not to say sour disillusion. It is unnecessary to appeal to the literature of educational dissent typified by such authors as Ivan Illich, Paul Goodman, John Holt and others of that ilk, in order to convince oneself that there is something seriously wrong with institutional schooling in its present form, when the best available research evidence points to conclusions scarcely less radical than theirs. The investigations of Coleman and Jencks into equality of educational opportunity (or rather the lack of it) in the U.S.A. and the surveys carried out by the International Association for the Evaluation of Educational Achievement in twenty different countries have consistently shown that social background and home conditions account for a major part of the differences in individual scholastic attainment and that schooling, by comparison, exercises a relatively minor influence. What it amounts to is that we have been expecting far too much of the schools: increasingly, they have been saddled with functions and responsibilities which were formerly discharged by other social agencies — family, Church, neighbourhood and work-place. Their failure to cope, though not their fault, now leaves them open to criticism and recrimination. As a consequence, the zeal for reform in the early 1960s, inspired by faith in the school as the seedbed for social justice, has been followed by a headlong retreat into cynical disavowal. In the event, the hopes placed originally in grandiose schemes and policies based on 'positive discrimination', for example the Educational Priority Area projects, have been sadly disappointed, and the realization that things have not turned out according to the intentions of the proponents of these and other reforms is not softened by the belated admission that when all is said and done the impossible takes a little longer. Not surprisingly, 'innovation', so recently on everyone's lips, is now well on the way to becoming a dirty word. Teachers, parents, politicians — all are weary of, and bewildered by, the non-stop changes that have been taking place. Enthusiasm for the cause of educational reform, to put it mildly, is at a low ebb.

As an OECD report observes:

> When the considerable expansion of educational facilities was envisaged a decade ago, it was more or less assumed that by making more facilities available and distributing them properly in the right neighbourhoods and areas, there would be a marked change in the social composition of student bodies, and in the flow of people from less favoured classes into secondary schools and into higher education institutions. This has not happened to the degree expected.[1]

It is as though education had been tried and found wanting. From less than two per cent of the Gross National Product in 1944, the proportion devoted to the educational services has risen to 7.5 per cent in 1976, say the critics, the inference being that this escalation of expenditure has some kind of law of diminishing returns built into it. Financial cutbacks being necessary anyway, the temptation is to look for scapegoats — and education is usually the first to be picked upon.

In order to understand what is happening in the current debate on the state of British education it is worthwhile taking a look at the polarization of opinion in other countries, if only for the sake of reassuring ourselves that the issues raised and the problems whch generate most heat in that debate are neither peculiar to Britain nor confined to it. The remarkable transformation which has occurred on the American scene since 1970 is reviewed by Fred Hechinger in a book with the provocative title *Murder in Academy: The Demise of Education*, in which he points out that the situation in the U.S.A. is critical, if not positively alarming, in the sense that for the first time education is now under attack from both left-wing and right-wing factions. As he says, 'In the past, when education had to ward off only the attacks of the reactionary right the consequences were confined to occasional short-term setbacks. Popular faith in each generation's capacity to do better than its predecessor was inseparably linked to education as, in Horace Mann's words, the "Great Equalizer" and "society's balance wheel"'[2]. This link, he fears, may now be broken and popular faith in education exposed as a cruelly deceptive myth.

In West Germany, likewise, school reform is decidedly out of favour: according to Hellmut Becker, everyone from the Federal Chancellor himself down to the caretaker of the humblest Berufsschule is sick and tired of hearing about it. 'Both left and right agree on this. The far left thinks that school reform in the first place was never really intended, in the second place has not occurred, and if it ever had occurred would have been an instrument for reinforcing the power of the ruling class'[3]. Becker notes that this polarization of political ideologies is rendered the more striking by the fact that although the arguments used by the two sides are contradictory their dissatisfaction is shared.

In a catastrophe set of the kind analysed by René Thom the lines of force are drawn so as to cause points in the three-dimensional graph curve where sudden discontinuities are liable to occur. A soap bubble swells and bursts, a man drops dead from a heart attack, a firm goes bankrupt. Not that all 'catastrophes' are as final and irreversible as these. Even the most abstruse topological calculation cannot predict when they are likely to occur or what form they will take, but even if only in a very general way, Thom's theory can be helpful in setting the parameters for such apparent discontinuities. To put it less melodramatically, in a situation of unbearable stress, as when an individual, an education system or even a whole nation is subjected to powerful and opposed forces of attraction and repulsion, the tendency is to fly from one extreme to another. Caught between the impulses of rage and fear, the cornered dog either snarls and rushes to the attack or retreats whimpering with its tail between its legs. The difficulty is to decide what tips the balance one way or the other.

Whether we are content to say that British education is merely suffering from a temporary setback or take the gloomier view that it has come to the end of an era and is now entering what Thomas Kuhn described as a phase of 'crisis' in which 'shoddy science' is the rule both in its theory and practice, makes little difference: either way, the indications are that it is so far down the slippery slopes of recession that no upturn in its fortunes can be expected in the foreseeable future. Long the darling of the progressives, it is now in danger of becoming the whipping boy of a vindictive *arrière-garde*, whose cry is, 'Back to the Three Rs and all that'. It seems only the other day that top priority was being demanded for measures to combat an acute shortage of teachers; now, thanks to the fact that officials in the Department of Education and Science contrived to get their sums so hope-lessly wrong in the first place, thousands of newly qualified teachers look like being permanently unemployed and many Colleges of Education are to be closed down. Accident-prone planning, to be sure, is not confined to the educational field. The point about this example is that except by those whose livelihood depends upon keeping them open, the closure of the Colleges appears to have been accepted without a peep of protest, even hailed with glee by certain sections of a hostile press. A leader-writer in the *Daily Telegraph* (16 November 1976) goes so far as to urge the total abolition of teacher-training — as good an indication as any of the recent about-turn in educational thought and the willingness to put back the clock.

Since 1973, when one by one the traffic lights turned red and the educational boom was abruptly brought to a halt, policy-making has found itself impaled on the horns of a dilemma not unlike that of Thom's cornered dog. Should it stand still and maintain the *status quo* as best it can in the hope that the situation will ease sooner or later? Not a chance. Should it conclude that the evidence of a law of diminishing returns operating in the system is so convincing that there is nothing for it but to cut its losses and embark on a policy of retrenchment? Or should it intensify the search for alternative forms of organized learning and more effective means of deploying resources of manpower and finance?

'The indispensable remoulding of education demands that all its elements — theory and practice, structure and methods, management and organisation — be completely rethought from one and the same point of view', as the Faure Commission affirmed in their report *Learning To Be*. Brave words, but how to translate the rhetoric of this stern imperative into everyday practice? 'Education must shift into the future tense', says Alvin Toffler[4]. 'Now the past, to all intents and purposes, no longer exists', says John Vaizey[5]. But the past, alas, is heavy on our backs, the present is confused, and the future looks bleak. All in all, it is not a good time to be writing a retrospective account of developments in British education in the post-war era!

On the face of things it may appear that the swing to the right will continue and that a policy of retrenchment must ensue. It is easy to forget that popular commitment to the cause of education is a fairly recent phenomenon in British society and that there is no guarantee that it will persist. Almost invariably, the liberal reforms of the nineteenth century were pioneered by minority groups, more often than not in the face of stiff opposition from public opinion. Churchill, for one, was disinclined to support proposals for a new Education Bill when they were first mooted in 1941-42, and not simply because he was heavily preoccupied with prosecuting the war effort: 'Your main task at present is to get the schools working as well as possible', he told the President of the Board of Education in a curt memorandum — a sentiment which would probably be endorsed by any Prime Minister today. Gosden notes that

possibly the greatest contrast between the prewar and postwar situation was the much greater willingness of central and local authorities to spend far more on education in real terms — in spite of economic policies of stop-go. The predominant attitude came to be one of expecting a measure of growth in expenditure from one year to another. The predominant prewar attitude had been one of containment of, or an actual reduction in, expenditure. This change was no doubt a reflection of changed social and political values as a consequence of the war.[6]

It is at any rate conceivable now that the continuous growth-curve in educational expenditure has been arrested that we are about to witness a return to pre-war attitudes towards policy-making.

In general, however, the period has been characterized by a number of basic trends which can safely be projected into the future. Dominant among these has been the drive for equality of opportunity, an ideal capable of widely differing interpretations. Unquestionably, this drive has gathered its political momentum from the rise in levels of aspiration and expectation on the part of the masses, in particular of the younger generation, who are more apt to question authority than their predecessors ever dared to do, who insist on the right to participation in the decision-making process, and who favour a more open institutional framework than the one imposed upon them by a bureaucratic system. At the same time, the period has been notable for the steady increase in state control of the education system at all points. It is for this reason that thinkers like Torsten Husén warn that schools as now constituted are on a collision course with society.

Back in 1944, when the present author was writing *Education in England*, he quoted two of the most eminent planners of the day, first F.A. Hayek: 'We can, unfortunately, not extend the sphere of common action and still leave the individual free in his own sphere. Once the communal sector, in which the state controls all the means, exceeds a certain proportion of the whole, the effect of its actions is to dominate the whole system'; the second, Karl Mannheim:

The only way in which a planned society differs from that of the nineteenth century is that more and more spheres of social life, and ultimately each and all of them, are subjected to state control. But if a few controls can be held in check by parliamentary sovereignty so can many .... In a democratic State sovereignty can be boundlessly strengthened by plenary powers without renouncing democratic control.

Looking back, it is easy to conclude that the second of these contradictory social theories has been the more influential in bringing British education to its present pass.

Certainly, developments flowing from the 1944 Education Act were motivated by a strong belief in the power of school reform to bring about social reform on the one hand and economic growth on the other. On both counts this belief has been seriously undermined during the past decade. As regards the first, it seems pertinent to remark that even if it could be proved that schooling *per se* exercises a relatively insignificant influence this would be no excuse for dismissing it as unimportant. In fact, the research evidence on the effects of formal schooling, plausible as it is, remains as contentious and open to different interpretations, as the research evidence on the relationship between genetic endowment and environmental influences in human make-up. Supposing that it could be shown conclusively (which it cannot) that eighty per cent of a person's intelligence — whatever that is taken as meaning — was determined by the parental genes at the moment of conception and that nothing could be done to change it subsequently, this would be all the more reason for concentrating on those aspects of the environment which are capable of being changed. By the same token, if it could be shown that eighty per cent of a person's life chances are attributable to social background and home conditions, this would be an argument for reinforcing, not relaxing, the work of the schools.

The evident failure of expansionist policies to produce the expected economic returns is the more puzzling, seeing that the failure is largely restricted to Britain. Without necessarily thinking that fifty-odd developing countries cannot be wrong in believing that the educational enterprise is wealth-creating, why should the validity of theories of 'investment in human capital' be called in question? The answer can only be that in their more naive applications — as in the British expansionist policies in recent years — such theories can have disastrous consequences. Says Peter Drucker, from whose book the title of this preamble is borrowed, 'There are few areas where right action depends so much on right theory as it does in economics. Yet in few areas is accepted theory as inadequate to the demands of practice and policy or to what we know.'

What little we do know can be gathered by comparing the educational and economic records of West Germany and the United Kingdom in the post-war period, as well as those of the U.S.A. Whereas in the U.K. the reorganization of secondary schools on non-selective lines has proceeded apace along with massive increases in the number of university students, new foundations, polytechnics and the rest, the West German system has remained for the most part traditional in character, retaining its highly selective Gymnasium, its *numerus clausus* for would-be university entrants, while providing vocational and apprenticeship courses for the majority of school-leavers. Result: in the first case, near-bankruptcy; in the second, all-round affluence. When asked how he explained this extraordinary discrepancy in the fortunes of the two countries a former Federal Minister of Education confided, not entirely in jest, that German politicans had never been so foolish as to imagine that there was much, or any, connection between educational reform and economic growth. The real explanation, one suspects, is a good deal more complex and has something to do with the fact that the Germans, like the Japanese, are a highly disciplined people, accustomed to hard work, to obeying orders, and who see nothing objectionable in a system which slots them into the requirements of the labour market at an early age.

In the U.S.A., where theories of investment in human capital first gained credence, the accent, by contrast, has always been on free enterprise and individual choice. Despite Jencks's conclusion that occupational status is largely a matter of luck, it is probably true that most Americans still believe that education 'pays', that it is a commodity which it is impossible to have too much of, and that the economist's tables purporting to show that a Ph.D. will result in greater life earnings than the possession of a first degree and so on, can, on the whole, be trusted. As a hard-headed, businesslike people, moreover, they can hardly be faulted for doing so. The truth is that American culture, unlike British, has never been saddled with class-conscious distinctions between 'pure' and 'applied' studies, or between work-based courses and those based on the traditional academic disciplines. Given a free choice in an elective high school and college curriculum, the American student is just as likely to opt for driver education, mining technology or food processing as he is for physics or history. In this way, a balance is preserved between the needs of material 'production' and the ever-increasing service sector of the labour market.

So far as Britain is concerned, any failure on the part of the education system to deliver the goods is better ascribed to the climate of opinion rather to an inherent fault in theories of investment in human capital. It is easy to see what would happen if a majority of young people were conditioned to believe that certain courses of study, say fine art, English literature and Latin, carried greater prestige than others like electrical engineering, veterinary surgery and public hygiene. Yet this, or something like it, is the way in which most of them *have* been conditioned. Given a free choice in the prevailing climate of opinion, the chances are that too many of them will prefer to follow courses leading to academic qualifications which bear little relation to the requirements of the labour market and which that market cannot absorb. As the Chairman of the Schools Council has rightly remarked, for every engineer needed in Britain today we now have a dozen unemployable sociologists. If the German way seems reminiscent of Hayek's *Road to Serfdom*, the British liking for muddling through policies and the dislike of any suggestion of the need for manpower planning begin to look suspiciously like a rake's progress.

Not that there has been any lack of plans affecting different sectors of the educational field: on the contrary, hindsight suggests that it has been a case of too many cooks. As happened

in the early days of 'alphabet soup' curriculum development in
the U.S.A. and Britain, these plans have sought to move one
piece at a time without much or any reference to the other pieces
on the board and without any overall view of the game as a
whole. Walter Perry puts his finger on the trouble when he says
that

> In the UK almost every requirement of the total educational
> system has been scrutinised by government committees with a
> view to introducing such modifications. The tragedy is that an
> overall philosophy to provide a framework for change has
> never been defined and accepted, with the result that the
> modifications actually introduced have been random rather
> than designed. A host of good ideas is buried in the reports
> the numerous committees — Plowden, Crowther, Hazelgrave,
> Robbins, James and Russell — which, if carefully selected and
> integrated, could provide much of the basis for a splendid
> new structure of educational provision.[7]

Francis Gladstone voices precisely the same criticism of post-war
urban developments — plenty of plans but no overview of what
planning should represent. The tactics exist, but not the stra-
tegy: and the outcome, by and large, is a comprehensive mess,
he thinks[8].

Too scathing a judgement? No doubt many would agree that
the reorganization of our secondary schools both before and after
the controversial Circular 10/65 (1965) is aptly described as a
'comprehensive mess'. They forget that the same accusations of
falling standards and a 'flight from scholarship' were levelled
against the American high school by critics of the calibre of
Admiral Rickover, James Bestor and Albert Lynd in the early
1950s, and that the American high school, despite some acute
growing pains, has subsequently put its house in order. They
forget that it is less than a decade since the enlightened approach
to learning and teaching in the primary schools of Oxfordshire,
Leicestershire and the West Riding of Yorkshire was admired by
visitors from all parts of the world. To deny the solid achievements of the past thirty-odd years would be stupid.

A Rip Van Winkle who fell asleep in the England of 1944

would be astonished and bewildered by the multifarious changes in social life and affairs which he could not fail to notice on awakening today. Certainly, a random list of the artefacts of contemporary British culture would be very different from the one sketched by T.S. Eliot in his *Notes towards a Definition of Culture*. The list would include such items as blue jeans, the Pill, high-rise flats, nylon tights, bingo halls, discos and super-markets, parking meters and traffic wardens, flyovers and motor-ways, jet aircraft and package holidays, transistors, tape recorders, hi-fi and pocket calculators, decimal coinage and metrication, oil rigs, computers and lasers, coloured immigrants, hippies, freak-outs and long-haired youths, canned beer and bearded men. Changes in dress alone might make it difficult for Rip to recognize half the people he met as his fellow countrymen. Changes in language usage would be no less mystifying, as would the fact that the pound in his pocket was now worth only a few pence.

And if Rip happened to be an educationist he would find the institutional landscape equally unfamiliar. Just as he would be left wondering what became of the half-crown, the florin, the sixpence and threepenny pieces he might well ask what had happened to the Central Advisory Councils, the Technical High Schools and County Colleges, all of which promised to be growth-points at the time he fell asleep. Comprehensive and Middle Schools, Polytechnics and Colleges of Education, the Open University, Teachers' Centres and Resource Centres (what on earth was meant by 'non-book materials' he might inquire?), the Schools Council, O- and A-levels and C.S.E. — these and a host of others had made their appearance during his slumbers. Doubtless he would be impressed by some of the changes, appalled by others, and hard put to decide whether the last state was better or worse than the first. On the other hand, he might count it a blessing that the life-styles in a permissive society were more carefree and less puritanical than those which the con-straints of post-war austerity had allowed. On the other, he might be tempted to think that there had been a general erosion of values, symbolized by the mutation of £sd into L.S.D. in the minds of many of the younger generation. *Autres temps, autres moeurs* ..., perhaps — or were they really 'different animals'?

Although the method of 'tracing history backwards' is no longer fashionable, then, it may be timely to look back without anger or nostalgia and trace the course of events which has led to the present hang-up. If it does nothing more, such a review may serve to remind us that if the educational machine looks like grinding to a halt it is not because it has run out of steam but because the way ahead is temporarily blocked by obstacles which are really not of its own making. Does anyone doubt that the Opec decision to treble the price of oil overnight precipitated the present crisis of confidence and that if it had not been taken it would still be a case of business as usual? Would the allegations of falling standards have been made so readily in a climate of opinion unworried by a sinking pound and by Britain's declining status as a world power? In fact, the allegations are easy to make but extraordinarily difficult to prove. So far as reading is concerned, a critical review of six regional and national research surveys carried out between 1966 and 1972 reports that 'No justification was found for a belief that standards are declining'[9]. The findings of the Bullock report more or less confirmed this: the general picture was one of rising reading scores through the 1950s and 1960s with a slight decline in the average score by 1970. Certainly, at the age of eleven no significant change in reading standards over the decade 1960-70 emerged from the N.S.6 test survey. Since it is unrealistic to expect eleven-year-olds, or any other age group, to become more proficient readers in successive generations, it may be thought that there is no cause for anxiety here. Less reassuring, of course, was the disclosure of widespread functional illiteracy in the adult population and possibly a growing proportion of poor readers among children of unskilled and semi-skilled parentage. The report rightly acknowledged that the validity of even the most up-to-date standardized test was affected by the passage of time, and that any findings needed to be treated with caution, a warning which did not prevent such findings being publicized in alarmist terms. Indeed, the closer the evidence is scrutinized, the more it begins to appear that rumours of falling standards are as ill-founded as those of thirty years ago when leading psychologists were convinced that the level of national intelligence was declining. As we know, the Scottish mental surveys in 1932, 1947 and 1956 allayed any fears on this score. All things considered, it seems more reasonable to suppose that standards of scholastic attainment are steadily rising: how else to explain the fact that a schoolgirl nowadays may need three or four O-levels in order to get a job as a shop assistant and that the requirements for entry into any kind of occupation are stepped up year by year? The 'diploma disease', so ably diagnosed by Ronald Dore, blights the entire learning process from start to finish, so much so that the whole purpose of attending school tends to be focussed on the passing of examinations — and is to that extent miseducative[10].

One of the less pleasing aspects of the current debate on the future of British education stems from the miasma of sour recrimination in which it is being conducted, the effect being to create a kind of smear campaign. Each of the contending parties seeks to discredit the others and is not over scrupulous in its efforts to do so. Since the big noises of the Left and Right are not on speaking terms, confrontation takes the place of fair-minded and informed discussion. The silent majority, apparently, has nothing to say. Granted, the prospects are grim, though nothing like so grim as those which the architects of the 1944 Education Act had to face during the dark days of the blitz. The pity of it is that the opportunity for creating a 'splendid new structure of educational provision' is there for the taking and that we lack the political will to grasp it resolutely.

Some of the disputes aroused in 1976 were so ill-tempered as to present the spectacle of nation bent on tearing itself apart. For the first time, a Secretary of State was found guilty of 'acting unreasonably'. Normally, that verdict would be accepted as unimpeachable: unfortunately, the situation in which we find ourselves is far from normal in the sense that the authority of the law itself is openly challenged so that it remains to be seen whether the Minister, the Tameside local education authority or the Law Lords will be proved to be wrong in the event. The same is true of the miserable William Tyndale *cause célèbre*, the case of a school whose staff, parents, managers and local authority actually succeeded in tearing it apart. Idle to suppose that the

rights and wrongs of such an unseemly affair could be finally
settled by calling in a Queen's Counsel to adjudicate.

The biased, not to say sensational reporting of Dr Bennett's
findings from his team research into the effects of different
teaching styles — findings which were relatively innocuous in
themselves but quickly seized on by the anti-progressive lobby
on the principle that any stick is good enough to beat a dog with
— and the referring back for further consideration of the Schools
Council's proposals for a common leaving certificate examination offer further examples of disputes in which it is hard to
decide which of the parties concerned is really 'acting unreasonably'. Between them, they illustrate the complex forces at
work and provide the context for any review of developments
leading up to them.

Clearly we have come to a pause. It is a time for serious second
thoughts. A cooling-off period awaits us. What better preparation for futurological speculation than to reflect on the trends
which have brought us to our present quandary?

References

1 *Economics of Education* (O.E.C.D., 1971), p.13.
2 F. Hechinger, *Murder in Academy: the Demise of Education*.
3 H. Becker, article in *Die Zeit*, June 1976.
4 A. Toffler, *Future Shock* (Pan Books edn, 1973), p.383.
5 J. Vaizey, foreword to G. Fragnière (ed.), *Education Without Frontiers* (Duckworth, 1976).
6 P.H.J.H. Gosden, *Education in the Second World War* (Methuen, 1976), p.433.
7 W. Perry, *The Open University* (Open University Press, 1976), p.1.
8 F. Gladstone, *The Politics of Planning* (Temple Smith, 1976).
9 E. Burke and D.G. Lewis, 'Standards of reading: a critical review of some recent studies', *Educational Research*, vol. 17, no. 3.
10 R. Dore, *The Diploma Disease* (Allen & Unwin, 1976, *passim*.

2 The continuous process – primary education

In an ideal world the primary importance of primary education would be taken as self-evident. Whether or not it be true that childhood was first 'discovered' in the late seventeenth century, wise parents and understanding teachers have always recognised the truth of Rousseau's saying, '*Le plus dangereux intervalle de la vie humaine est celui de la naissance jusqu'à l'âge de douze ans*', but in general this recognition of the crucial nature of the early years as the most formative period in the educational process has received more lip service than active support. In the imperfect world in which schools operate, this stage has been granted rather less attention and more niggardly resources than those devoted to secondary and higher education. With the solitary exception of the 11-plus selection procedures, the issues raised in it have usually tended to be less vexatious, with the result that only rarely has it found itself in the spotlight of publicity. Significantly, the 1944 Act referred to it in terms which were nothing if not vacuous: 'that is to say, full-time education suitable to the requirements of junior pupils', the latter being classified in Section 114 as children who had not attained the age of twelve years. As revised in the Education (Miscellaneous Provisions) Act, 1948, this non-definition was left open to even vaguer interpretations: 'full-time education suitable to the requirements of junior pupils who have not attained the age of ten years and six months, and full-time education suitable to the requirements of junior pupils who have attained that age and whom it is expedient to educate together with pupils who have not attained that age'. Such legal verbiage, it may be thought, only served to confirm the primary stage as that part of the educational process left over from a truncated elementary school system. Any meaning which might be attached to the 'requirements of junior pupils' or to what might be 'suitable' and 'expedient' means of satisfying them, was left completely in the air. Significantly, too, both the 1931 Hadow Report on *Primary Education* and the 1967 Plowden Report on *Children and their Primary Schools* were in the nature of afterthoughts in the sense that both followed reports concerned with the reorganization of secondary schools.

Thank goodness, then, for our little infants' schools and for the British practice of sending children to school a year earlier than is thought 'expedient' in most other countries. Thanks also to the peculiarly English arrangement by which 5-7-year-old boys and girls are often accommodated in buildings apart from their older brethren, insulated from the 'serious business' of schooling. Despite the inspired example set by the McMillan sisters in the Deptford slums, the provision of nursery schools and nursery classes remained so scandalously inadequate throughout the inter-war years that as late as 1939 there were more Ecoles Maternelles and Classes Enfantines in the Pas de Calais alone than there were in the whole of England and Wales. As the Board of Education confessed: 'Beginning in 1918 with 13 schools the number had risen by 1923 to 24 schools, 10 provided by local education authorities and 14 by voluntary bodies. There was, however, little further progress owing to the necessity for economy until 1931 when the total was only 30'[1]. That the situation is little better today and that the same lame excuses for relegating the unfinished business of pre-school education to the limbo of lost causes may be taken as reflecting on our backwardness as a nation.

But if nursery schools were pitiably few and far between, the lessons learned in them did not go unheeded: they pointed the way which at least some of the more enlightened infants' schools followed. It seems idle to suppose that in doing so they were influenced to any great extent either by Froebelian principles or by the new developmental psychology. Few two-year certificated women teachers, one imagines, were familiar with the ideas of Dewey, fewer still with the work of Piaget. Practical rather than theoretical considerations led them to adopt what later came to be called a child-centred approach: just why will be readily appreciated by anyone who has tried talking to very young children. Because adult language is literally over his head the baby is *unteachable* in the sense that he cannot or does not respond to formal instruction. The word of command is more likely to be ignored than it is to be obeyed. Wide open as he is to suggestion and indoctrination, the infant goes his own way, blissfully immune to the dictates of his would-be mentors. In the nursery classroom or the play group, as in the intimacy of the mother-child relationship, it soon becomes apparent that the teacher's first duty is to observe the learner's behaviour, something he cannot do until he has rid himself of the illusion that he understands perfectly how the youngster's mind works. In the process he (normally she!) sooner or later arrives at the conclusion that his/her main function is not to impart information by means of formal instruction but to encourage self-activity, to stimulate interest, and rarely to forbid or suppress impulses even when these seem wholly undesirable to adult ways of thinking.

This, broadly, was the more permissive approach to learning and teaching, stemming originally from a handful of nursery and infants' schools, which has provided the secret leaven, permeating upwards from the lower age levels, in English primary education during the post-war era. However fitfully and sporadically, child-centred theory and practice infiltrated from the reception classes of infants' schools and departments into the junior schools, thence into the lower reaches of the secondary modern school. Although it was met at all points with stiff opposition, nowhere more powerfully than in Scotland where its influence was delayed for thirty years or more, it is hardly an exaggeration to claim that every significant advance in British education can be traced back to this source. Today, when the outcry alleging falling standards in the 'basic subjects' is once again being raised, such a claim, difficult as it is to substantiate, needs to be defended more stoutly than ever.

The origins of child-centredness

To be sure, there was no single source. Child-centred theory has a long and respectable intellectual history dating back at least to the *Great Didactic* of Comenius and finding its expression in a school of thought represented by a line of 'Great Educators' from Rousseau, Pestalozzi and Froebel down to Montessori and John Dewey. Before 1900, however, its effects on practice were minimal, ruled out by the bleak conditions prevailing in the elementary schools which were slow in recovering from the effects of Payment by Results. Prompted by what George Bernard Shaw called 'a sense of struggle against the prison morality of our schools', a small and curiously mixed *avant-garde* group joined the international movement in favour of progressive education before, during and after the 1914-18 war. Among the leading figures in it were Beatrice Ensor, Homer Lane (ultra-radical founder of the Little Commonwealth), Albert Mansbridge and R.H. Tawney (representing the Workers' Educational Association), the McMillan sisters, Norman MacMunn, the one and only A.S. Neill, and Edmond Holmes, whose book *What Is and What Might Be*, published in 1911, testified to the need for a more liberal and humane outlook on the part of the Inspectorate. After 1921, the patient campaigning of the New Educational Fellowship was certainly not without influence. The extent of the spin-off from John Dewey's influence is more difficult to assess but it has been reckoned that in the 1920s as many as 1,500 English schools were working on Helen Parkhurst's Dalton Plan as compared with only 200 in America[2]. Carleton Washburne's Winnetka Plan, according to which individual pupils were responsible for mastering the units of achievement assigned to them, proved to be less popular in Britain; not so W.H. Kilpatrick's 'Project Method' which was soon to be featured in many schools, albeit in debased forms of which Dewey himself would have disapproved.

No less seminal were the empirical findings of child-study, so well exemplified by Susaan Isaacs' daringly experimental and short-lived Malting House School in the 1920s and subsequently in her capacity as Director of the newly established Department of Child Development at the London University Institute of Education. Long before Piaget was a name to conjure with, the prolific writings of Susan Isaacs, a nice blend of womanly intuition and the 'new psychology', helped to create a fresh climate of opinion in the two-year training colleges. As one of her associates and disciples explained:

> The emotional life of the children makes an even more difficult problem. Our chief concern is to produce a new generation less nerve-ridden than the old. The newest psychology has taught us something about what to avoid in the way of repression, what kinds of attachment should be encouraged and what discouraged, what sort of emotional outlets should be provided. This knowledge is being acted upon as far as possible, and new light looked for from the observation of this group of children.

> I will come now to what is actually done in the school. The best way to prepare a person for life is to safeguard his zest for life. The Malting House children certainly have it. When I first came to the school I tried to decide what was the most striking differences between this school and any other I have known. I came to the conclusion that it is the happiness of the children. Not that I have not been in happy schools. But I have never seen so much pleased concentration, so many shrieks and gurgles of joy as here. Of course this joy is particularly apparent because its expresison is not hindered. If you want to dance with excitement you may ....

> I suppose the reason for this happiness is that there is plenty of space, that material equipment is abundant and suitable, and that the child is free to use it in ways that appeal to him,

instead of being forced to do with it those things which his elders consider good for him. It is delightful to be in a school where the usual answer to the question, 'May we do so-and-so?' is 'Yes', instead of the almost automatic 'No' one finds oneself expecting.[3]

No résumé of the rise and progress of the child-centred movement of ideas would be complete, either, if it omitted the name of Sir Percy Nunn, first Director of the London Institute of Education and the man responsible for Susan Isaacs' appointment. His *Education: Its Data and First Principle, Intelligence and Character*, remained essential reading for intending teachers, graduate as well as non-graduate, for many years. Taking its stand on the position that nothing good enters this world except through the free activities of individual human beings, Nunn's 'horme' and 'mneme' (archaic-sounding terms to the contemporary reader) championed the cause of those who sought to safeguard the young learner's 'zest for life'. As an educational theory it owed as much to Freudian libido as it did to Bersonian *élan vital*. A similar spirit was evinced by the revelations in child act popularized by Cizek and Viola and in the 'modern dance' of Rudolf Laban.

All of this found its official expression in the 1931 Report on *The Primary School* with its famous pronouncement that 'the Curriculum is to be thought of in terms of activity and experience rather than of knowledge to be acquired and facts to be stored'. Assailed as it has been as a woolly document on the ground that it left the door open to a host of vague concepts such as 'readiness', 'free expression', 'growth' and 'maturation', etc., which led to the adoption of sloppy methods of teaching, Sir Alec Clegg, for one, is disposed to think that history may yet decide it to be 'the most significant educational report of the first half of the present century'[4]. By comparison, certainly, the much blowsier Plowden Report (1967) and the ca' canny *Primary Education in Scotland* (1965) offered no more than a belated reaffirmation of the general principles enunciated by the Consultative Committee of the Board of Education thirty-odd years earlier.

No doubt the language of Hadowism *was* turgid and its view of the conditions prevailing in most schools more optimistic and realistic, but at least it was correct in seeing the primary curriculum as evolving through three overlapping phases of development. Initially, the aim had been to teach children to read 'if only for the best of purposes, that they may read the Scripture' — writing was at first actually discouraged since it might induce 'a disrelish for the laborious occupations of life'. During the second phase, the regimen imposed by the Revised Code after 1870, the more or less exclusive concern was to assure minimum standards of proficiency in reading, writing and arithmetic — the so-called 'basic subjects'. A third phase as envisaged by the Hadow Committee was now in the process of transforming this older and primitive tradition of elementary schooling.

> During the last forty years, and with increasing rapidity in the twelve years since 1918, the outlook of the primary school has been broadened and humanized. Today it includes care, through the school medical service, for the physical welfare of children, offers larger, if still inadequate, opportunities for practical activity, and handles the curriculum, not only as consisting of lessons to be mastered, but as providing fields for new and interesting experience to be explored; it appeals less to passive obedience and more to the sympathy, social spirit and imagination of children, relies less on mass instruction and more on the encouragement of individual and group work, and treats the school, in short, not as the antithesis of life, but as its complement and commentary.[5]

As a prescription for what-might-be, this overblown sentence, worthy of Sir Walter Scott in fully cry, typified the wishful forward-thinking of the 1930s. For all that, it heralded all-round changes in the ethos of English primary schools — 'open-plan', 'integrated day' and the rest — which could hardly have been anticipated at the time. Although most schools continued to operate on the old Herbartian-Gradgrind lines, here and there adventurous teachers were endeavouring to translate the 'activity and experience' theory into everyday practice. A common criticism, not altogether unfounded, has always been that such a theory is unworkable with large classes and in cramped classrooms. Catering for individual differences, it was often said (and still is), may be possible in the kind of ideal conditions enjoyed by the Malting House children, but not in state-maintained schools.

That such criticism was not unanswerable was triumphantly demonstrated in an H.M.S.O. publication *The Story of a School* (1949). Arising from makeshift projects in the early days of evacuation, Arthur Stone, headmaster of Steward Street Primary School, an antediluvian three-decker building in one of the seedier inner-city areas of Birmingham, had evolved a 'free expression', 'activity and experience' curriculum in which art, music, mime and dance were prominently featured.

At the risk of introducing a personal note, my impressions of a memorable visit to Steward Street in 1945 as recorded in *Purpose in the Junior School* are as quotable now as they were then:

> The school premises are old and dismal. The junior department is housed on the second floor of a barracks-style building originally meant to hold 250 pupils and now accommodating well over 300. There are 6 classrooms and a hall in which a complete assembly is barely possible. The worn staircase and rickety balustrade are far from inviting; and yet, somehow, immediately on entry one senses the cheeful, lively atmosphere of the place. The porch is decorated with naive wall-paintings, the work of 8-year-olds by the look of them, and the corridors are so covered with pattern-work that an otherwise stygian interior is irradiated with brightness and colour. The mass effect is bizarre, not to say startling, and more than gives a hint of coming excitements ....
>
> The Head explains that except for a 45 minute Arithmetic period each morning the time-table is completely fluid. In effect, there is no time-table. There are 3 Music and Dance periods, 4 for PT and one for Games, but these are not regarded as fixed points; they may be taken on different days at different times by mutual give-and-take between members of staff and the various classes. Teachers and children alike are

free to undertake activities as and when they feel inclined or as occasion demands. If, for any reason, a pupil loses interest or feels 'left out' there is nothing to prevent his opting out for an alternative of his own choosing, even if it means going off to another classroom. Roughly, the idea is that children can only give of their best when they are completely absorbed, and that if they are not in the mood for singing, say, it is better not to insist upon it.

This school has a philosophy which might be summed up in the phrase: 'Freedom from fear of failure', in that nothing is attempted until and unless the individual pupil is seen to be ready and eager to learn.[6]

More so than any of the official reports which preceded it, *The Story of a School* and the Ministry's film which accompanied its publication, not only helped to advertise 'progressive' methods: by seeming to set the seal of approval on them it gave them *carte blanche*. For the next twenty years the wind of change was set fair in favour of child-centred education. In 1947 Stone left Steward Street to join the West Riding as a County Council Inspector. Teachers in the area owed much to his guidance and leadership. Sir Alec Clegg, as tough-minded a Director of Education as any, but happily one with fire in his belly, makes the comment that

Those of us who were administering the service at the time and observing the schools suddenly saw the obvious, which was that all these expressive activities in art, drama, movement, and later in writing, had the same aim; children were being led into experiences which stimulated their powers of expression. The growth of the child as a personality was becoming more important than the teaching of separate, examinable subjects, and gradually it came about that every child mattered. Within a few years there were not two schools out of a thousand working in this way, but a score or more, and today it is hard to find a school that is not influenced in some way or another by the new ways.[7]

The possibility that 'progressive' methods might easily be

carried to excess by incompetent teachers was, of course, always recognized. Child-centredness as adumbrated in *Emile* or in Wordsworth's *Ode on Intimations of Immortality* was essentially romantic and might have been none the worse for that but for the fact that in ordinary mortals romanticism degenerates into insipid sentimentalism. At the turn of the century Margaret McMillan had felt it necessary to warn that even in the nursery school 'the opportunity for free expression is given often, *and always after drill*' [8]. Bearing in mind the modest accomplishments of the great majority of two-year college trained women — in 1962 only 2.5 per cent were graduates and six per cent of the 141,000 teachers serving in primary schools were non-certificated — it is hardly surprising that the warning often went unheeded:

> If the teacher does not realise that to teach thirty-five children as individuals and to meet their every need is an exacting task which needs much skill, sympathy, organising ability and above all an understanding of the way children grow and develop, there will be failure and some of it serious, and the harm done can be almost as great as when the last five in the mental arithmetic test are made to come out every day to have their inadequacy paraded. When a class seems happy but is totally lacking purpose it is no answer for the teacher to say with a winning smile, 'Ah, but we are doing a project' or 'All our work is open-ended', or worse still as one teacher put it, 'We are a muck and muddle school but we are all happy'. In such schools where work is lamentably undemanding the effect, as one visitor put it, is that of 'a wet play time all day'. [9]

But if, in places, the trend towards 'activity and experience' invited discredit, by 1950 the philosophy of child-centredness was well and truly in the ascendant. Its passionate concern for the 'whole child' was reflected in John Blackie's *Good Enough for the Children?* (1963), the kind of book which shines like a good deed in a naughty world and one which deserves to rank as a minor classic in the educational literature of the period. As if determined to let it be seen that his Chief Inspector's heart was in the right place, he relied less on arguments than on telling anecdotes, none more poignant than the story of a nine-year-old boy's composition entitled 'My real father' which ended thus:

> 'My father was very kind to me and gave me and my cousins cigarette cards. He likes doing woodwork, my father, for me, and he likes a little game of cards now and then; or a game of darts. He chops wood and saws the planks and he is a handsome man but he is dead. He worked at the rubber works before he died.'

— to which the teacher's comment had been, 'Tenses. You keep mixing past and present'[10].

Sentimentalism or sensitivity? Unlike the freedom allowable in child art, the vogue for 'creative writing' was constrained by a long-standing tradition of formal instruction in the rules of grammar and spelling. Authors like Blackie and David Holbrook, whose *English for the Rejected* pleaded for a relaxation of this rule-bound state of affairs, might gain a sympathetic hearing but their advocacy was bound to seem less than convincing to the majority of teachers who were usually left in no doubt that their main job was to ensure that as many of their pupils as possible passed the 11-plus examination. In short, a child-centred approach conflicted as much with the historical determinants or primary schooling as it did with the socioeconomic forces and interests which were hostile to its adoption.

The elementary school hangover

In his sociological description of English primary schools, W.A.L. Blyth discriminates between three traditions: (a) elementary, (b) preparatory and (c) developmental. Of these the first was always the most powerful in delimiting the schools' functions and in defining the roles of teachers and pupils. It may be remarked in passing that this tradition, a heritage from the bleak age of the Revised Code, is the one to which appeal is made by those who periodically profess to be alarmed about falling standards in the 'basic subjects'.

The lay-out of the nineteenth- and early twentieth-century

elementary classroom was designed on mass production lines and the school's structure itself modelled on the factory. Its not-so-hidden curriculum conditioned pupils to 'pay attention', to 'stop talking', to unquestioning obedience, to acceptance of corporal punishment, to punctuality, neatness, frugality, token rewards for hard work and other virtues which were held to be in keeping with their lowly station in life. To this day, many classrooms answer to this description:

> They sit in desks usually, often in rows, all facing one way, although contemporary furniture and classroom organisation is tending to change this. The basic grid of rows and aisles helps to define the area of attention somewhat and enables the teacher placed at the front of the class and usually with a somewhat higher desk, possibly a dais, to supervise the class and when necessary to became a focus of attention. The desk helps to indicate the sobriety of behaviour expected, the rows to show the neatness of planning and habits which teachers hope to see appearing in their pupils and the formation represents as a whole a 'unit' for class teaching and many teachers would feel uneasy if they had not these rows to deal with — they might consider that the classroom would then become slovenly and unbusinesslike, at least in appearance.[11]

Above all, the elementary classroom was a place for instruction. Lessons consisted mainly of teacher-talk with pupils answering questions at best intermittently and only when asked. Rote learning and drill methods occupied a good deal of the time. It was a lockstep system which took little or no account of individual differences: all were in the same 'standard' and supposed to progress at much the same rate. The curriculum was of the collection type, a very bareboned collection in which the three Rs were by far the most important ingredients, with smatterings of history, geography, nature study, drawing and singing thrown in by way of light relief — frills. Indoors or outdoors, physical training was performed as drill, a series of exercises done to numbers and in quasi-military fashion. Except in denominational schools, religious instruction took the form of

Bible stories, and the daily act of corporate worship, overtly beneficent in intention, also had the covert aim of reinforcing the dominant-submissive relationship between staff and pupils. In any case, not being regarded as an examinable subject, as time went on religious instruction tended to be more honoured in the breach than the observance!

All subjects were parcelled out in a time-table blocked out in lessons lasting thirty, forty-five or sixty minutes, each started and stopped by the peremptory school bell. Learning was conducted on mechanical lines, whether it meant chanting arithmetical tables in unison, going through the motions of P.T. or standing in lines in the playground when the whistle blew for admission to school each morning and afternoon.

But if formal instruction provided the be-all and end-all of its business, the elementary school was preeminently an institution for the socialization of children who were destined to be third-class citizens. It originated in a society in which rigid class distinctions were regarded as God-given and unalterable and it carried the stigmata of inferiority long after 1926 when the Hadow Committee decided that the very word 'elementary' had become so objectionable that the time had come to give it a decent burial. Unfortunately, the elementary tradition was singularly hard of dying. From the start, the children it catered for were of humble parentage — the 'multitude of laborious poor' as they were referred to in early Victorian times — and it was generally understood that in adult life most of them would follow menial or semi-skilled occupations. Accordingly, it was never intended that they should expect anything better. If not exactly nasty — so far as one can tell, most elementary schools appear to have been happy and industrious places for all their being so routine-ridden — the provision made for them was certainly cheap. As regards qualifications, status and salaries elementary schoolteachers were the lowest in the professional pecking order, a race apart, servants with no prospects whatever for upward mobility to join the ranks of grammar *schoolmasters*. Their pupils, likewise, got the same message: whatever else they learned, they learned not to think too highly of themselves.

The 11-plus and all that

Still, as the sage Dr Johnson remarked, 'Reading is nothing but rising in the world'. Like Oliver Twist, a generation reared on the frugal diet of the three Rs eventually plucked up courage enough to ask for more. As a self-contained system offering a terminal course leading straight into the world of work, the old elementary school had little need to exercise its classificatory function. After 1907, however, when for the first time a small percentage of its ten-year-old pupils were allocated to free places in grammar schools on the basis of a competitive examination, classification quickly came to be regarded as *the* function of the lower elementary school. Since the subjects tested in the examination were restricted to arithmetic ('mechanical' and 'problems') and written English (grammatical exercises and 'composition') the pressure on teachers and pupils to drop everything else became increasingly intense. Ambitious parents, anxious for their children's future, rated as best those schools which earned a reputation for producing the biggest number of 'scholarship' winners. In the bigger urban schools, streaming from an early age became the rule, with admission to the 'scholarship class' as the all-or-nothing goal set for pupils who were left in no doubt that any form of study not connected with the examination was a pointless waste of time.

So began the whole sorry, tangled business of the 11-plus, which has been a bone of contention in English education ever since. Any discussion of the conflicting ideologies involved in the selection for different types of secondary school is better left over for consideration in the next chapter: enough for the moment, to say that their ill effects were prejudicial to developments in the primary school. Since so much depended on achieving success in an examination which effectively decided each candidate's life-chances once and for all, since the borderline between success and failure was normally pitched so high that the great majority were doomed to be disappointed, and since time for preparation was so short, the stresses and strains experienced by all concerned vitiated and distorted the work of the junior schools and to some extent that of many infants' schools also. From the moment the five-year-old set foot inside the reception class, it is almost true to say, his work was cut out for him.

Admittedly, it is easy to exaggerate — and equally easy to assert that nine out of ten children took the examination in their stride. The fact that in many L.E.A.s nine out of ten were refused 'special places' and transferred to secondary modern schools, however, indicates that freedom from fear of failure was exceptional rather than the rule. In rural areas where the provision of grammar school places was adequate the stresses and strains of competition were often a good deal less severe than they were in the densely populated industrial towns. It was only after 1944, when fees were abolished in state-maintained secondary schools, that failure to win a place caused serious concern, even distress, among middle-class and aspiring working-class parents who would not afford to send their children to independent schools. As for those bracketed at the bottom of the Registrar General's list, the general attitude was one of indifference, so much so that as often as not the offer of a 'special place' was likely to be rejected. The alienation of large sections of the working class, typified by the Marburton youth's comment on his local grammar school, 'What a bloody way to grow up!', was so deeply ingrained that they might almost be said to have opted out of the 11-plus rat race.

In Scotland, where the age of transfer was normally fixed at twelve and where something like thirty-three per cent were admitted to academic Senior Secondary Schools, social discontent with selection procedures was less pronounced than in England. In retrospect, the 1926 decision in favour of a 'clean break' owed more to administrative convenience than it did to sound reasoning. The florid rhetoric of *The Education of the Adolescent* ('There is a tide which begins to rise in the veins of youth at the age of eleven or twelve') left the issue unresolved until the 1964 Education Act legalized departures from the established 5-11 pattern and opened the way for Middle Schools catering for the 8-12 or 9-13 age groups. In the independent preparatory schools the age of transfer had always been 13. Why not 12, then, as in Scotland? Rightly or wrongly, the English answer was that since 1907 transfers from elementary to grammar schools had been arranged on the basis of a competitive examination taken by pupils in their eleventh year, and that so long as the school-leaving age was fixed at 14 it would not be possible to organize anything like a full-length course for secondary-modern pupils if the age of transfer were to be later than 11.

Before 1950, the thought that decisions affecting the learner's future at so early an age were bound to be both premature and unreliable could hardly be said to have caused much public concern. Generally speaking, the need for selection was taken for granted, as was the fairness of selection procedures. It is tempting to say that this equanimity was due to sheer ignorance, seeing that most L.E.A.s were highly secretive about the procedures they adopted. The widespread use of standardized intelligence tests helped to offset the common and valid criticism that the 11-plus examination measured scholastic *attainment* rather than scholastic *ability* and to that extent equalized the chances of pupils who had not received any intensive preparation for the examination. Previously, it is fair to say, it was as easy for a teacher who was an old hand at taking the 'scholarship class' to guarantee a high proportion of 'passes' as it was for a circus animal-trainer to get a wagonload of monkeys to jump through paper hoops.

For hard-pressed administrators, faced with the ticklish problem of allocating 'special places' which were always in short supply, the Intelligence Quotient was a godsend. Here, it was thought, was an infallible, exact and objective yardstick *and* a perfect predictor of a pupil's future academic performance. By adding a third element to the examination in arithmetic and written English, the I.Q. test made it possible to claim that the selection procedure was not only above board but as carefully designed as human wit could make it.

So it was. Nevertheless, even among the ranks of the educational psychologists there were those who were profoundly uneasy about the indiscriminate, wholesale use of standardized intelligence tests. It was known, for example, that *no* test was entirely 'culture free' and that many favoured children from middle-class backgrounds. It was known, too, that test scores obtained at the age of eleven were not immutable and that, far from being exact, allowance had to be made for the possible margins of error inherent in them. Longitudinal studies, moreover, had thrown doubts on the predictive value of the tests. Fewer children of semi- and unskilled parents gained five or more O-level passes in the General Certificate of Education examination than children from other classes with the same measured intelligence at eleven — and far fewer survived to the A-level and degree stages. To make matters worse, it had been found that there was actually a tendency for the scores of manual workers' children to deteriorate between the ages of eight and eleven, a pointer to the depressing effects of the kind of schooling to which they had been subjected. Finally, Vernon's disclosure[12] that regular coaching (which took place in many schools), could boost I.Q. scores by as much as fifteen points provided one more item of evidence for those who detested the 11-plus and all it stood for and who argued the case for its abolition.

But if the psychologists were reluctant to come down firmly on the side of the abolitionists, the evidence amassed by sociologists helped to clarify what, for the public at any rate, had hitherto been an ill-informed and inconclusive controversy and to make it a political issue. As if making up for lost time after its arrested development during the first half of the century, British sociology weighed in after 1950 with a series of research-based studies all of which showed that socioeconomic factors were responsible for inequalities of opportunity to a much greater extent than had previously been suspected. D.V. Glass's *Social Mobility in Britain* (1954) drew attention to the split level in social status created by a bipartite system of selective and non-selective secondary schools. Olive Banks's *Parity and Prestige in English Secondary Education* (1955) analysed the dysfunctions arising from the historical development of elementary and grammar schools as separate systems, and contrasted the 'sponsored mobility' enjoyed by direct-grant and independent schools with the 'contest mobility' typified by the 11-plus examination in the unprivileged maintained sector. Yet another key text, arguably the most influential because of its timing, was *Social Class and Educational Opportunity* (1956) which reported an investigation carried out by Jean Floud, A.H. Halsey and F.M. Martin into the variables affecting results in the 11-plus examination in south-west Hertfordshire and Middlesbrough. As a preliminary study of the ecology of educational opportunity, it confirmed suspicions about the essential injustice of early selection which had often been aired but never substantiated. It showed that in both areas middle-class parents were more interested in their children's progress than those from working-class backgrounds — the 'achievement syndrome' which brought pressure to bear on the primary schools. On the other hand, such environmental factors as housing, income, etc., appeared to be less important in the more affluent south-west Hertfordshire area than in Middlesbrough where the successful pupils at each social level were distinguished by the relative material prosperity of their houses.

Ostensibly, the purpose of the 11-plus examination was to select pupils who were capable of benefiting from an extended academic course of secondary education. In reality it was a Procrustean device for allocating pupils according to the number of grammar-school places available in the locality. This quota varied so enormously from region to region that the chances of gaining a place often depended more on geographical luck than on the pupil's performance. Simply because the provision of grammar-school places was invariably lower in predominantly working-class areas than it was elsewhere, the working-class pupil needed to have a higher I.Q. and a higher over-all score in the 11-plus examination if he was to have any chance of succeeding. In some rural counties the pass rate was as high as fifty per cent, in the cities as low as ten per cent. A pupil taking the examination of one L.E.A. might be assessed as a failure while another with an identical score in an adjoining L.E.A. where the borderline happened to be slightly lower was allowed to pass. In the big conurbations, where boundaries between L.E.A.s marked off catchment areas with different quotas of grammar-school places, the difference between success and failure was occasionally decided by the street number of the house in which a pupil lived.

While acknowledging that the authorities did their level best to cope with anomalies of this sort, therefore, the arbitrary nature of selection procedures became more and more apparent. Thanks to the 'limited pool of ability' myth, a myth created and perpetuated by the grammar schools themselves, the assumption had always been that only a few above-average ability pupils were capable of pursuing an extended course of secondary education. Just what proporiton of the 11-plus school population *was* capable had never been decided: it just happened that so far as England was concerned (but not Wales or Scotland) the proportion worked out at around twenty per cent.

All the major official reports which followed — Crowther (1959), Newsom (1963), Robbins (1963) and Plowden (1967) — relied heavily on sociological evidence, and although only the last dealt specifically with primary schools, all served to give added impetus to an egalitarian drive which culminated in the 10/65 Circular and the adoption of the 'comprehensive principle'. Thereafter, as more and more L.E.A.s scrapped their selection procedures the pressure on primary schools was eased and a *modus vivendi* more in keeping with their kind of developmental or child-centred approach once more became possible. At its best, as in Leicestershire, Oxfordshire and the West Riding, it won the applause of visitors from the far corners of the earth, notably by American teachers who were impressed by the informality of 'integrated day' schemes, open-plan buildings and thriving junior-school communities in which teachers, auxiliaries, parents and children worked side by side. Silberman sang their praises in *Crisis in the Classroom*, utterly convinced that the grassroots were much greener on this side of the Atlantic. Some of the natives were not so sure.

Curriculum innovation: hors-d'oeuvre or dog's breakfast?

Both the elementary and the developmental traditions held that certain studies were unsuitable for young children, although they did so for different reasons. The one devised a starkly formal curriculum consisting of spelling, dictation, grammatical exercises, composition, recitation, reading, handwriting, tables, mental arithmetic, 'sums' and little else; the other favoured an informal, fluid curriculum based on beliefs about how children learn, and organized it in terms of 'projects' and 'centres of interest' rather than 'subjects'. Neither was future-referenced in the sense that it was not constrained by demands imposed upon it by the secondary school. By comparison, the preparatory tradition, catering as it did for a wealthier clientele and an older age group, was much more academically inclined. Its objectives were set for it by the Common Entrance examination, taken at the age of thirteen-plus, in which candidates were required to achieve at least a minimum level of scholarship in a range of studies including Latin, French, algebra, geometry, history and physical science. As Blyth remarks, 'To the elementary tradition, all these things were alien. They were suspected of interfering with the basic skills or, if admitted to the curriculum at all, they were treated in a jejune and unimaginative manner.' Nevertheless, he says,

> In areas in which junior schools have taken on something of the colouring of private schools, and especially where they regularly compete for places in direct-grant and independent schools whose entrance examinations make demands of the *hors-d'oeuvre* pattern, the preparatory tradition has continued to show some influence, while in the most culturally deprived areas, such as slum districts and some rural villages, the problems of ensuring a minimum of language and number skills adequate for social communication and for any kind of secondary education has given some impetus to the perpetuation of the elementary ethos. The developmental tradition, while embracing a considerable amount of the same skills and subject-matter, takes its stand rather on the readiness of children in the later primary years to be introduced to a wider heritage and to explore their environment (wherever it is) and their own capacities for individual and collective activity and creativity.
>
> The interplay of the three traditions results in some degree of variability in each area of the junior-school curriculum, and in the balance between the various curricular elements. [13]

'Variability' is the *mot juste*. The truth is that apart from the 'basic skills' no one can afford to dogmatize about what children should learn between the ages of five and eleven — or twelve or thirteen — a state of uncertainty compounded by the fact that the 'basic skills' required today are in many respects quite different from those of fifty years ago. In any case, the range of cognitive ability becomes progressively wider from the age of seven or eight onwards, so that one pupil may be 'ready' to tackle infinitesimal calculus while another in the same class still cannot do his long-division sums in simple arithmetic. The problems of devising a common-core course which have pre-occupied curriculum development at the secondary stage in recent years are scarcely less intractable in junior and middle schools where they have received considerably less attention.

Once the bugbear of the 11-plus was safely out of the way, however, the way was left open for experiment. To date, unfortunately, such pilot ventures as have been attempted can only be characterized as piecemeal and ineffectual. One of the more ambitious and systematically planned sought to introduce the teaching of French to eight-year-olds and enjoyed something of a vogue during the early 1960s. Backed by audiovisual learning materials sponsored by the Nuffield Foundation at a cost of £100,000 and by intensive courses of in-service training organized by the D.E.S., primary French got off to a promising start in many areas, only to lose its momentum towards the end of the decade. While it is too early for it to be written off as abortive, this venture into new territory cannot be said to have made much headway and looks like coming to a dead end. In Glasgow, where closed-circuit television was used to provide a support system for teachers who knew little or no French, the results were profoundly disappointing, conceivably one reason why the city's elaborate E.T.V. service was the first to fall victim to financial cuts.

Schemes for the conversion of mechanical arithmetic into 'pure mathematics' involving symbolic problem-solving through the use of number series, the language of sets and topological concepts have also run into difficulties, as have others which seek to replace nature study by experimental science. The principles underlying these innovative projects were sound enough, ably expounded in the Curriculum Bulletins issued by the Schools Council: the trouble was that whether it was French, mathematics or science, most primary teachers simply did not have the necessary academic qualifications which would have enabled them to cope with the sudden changes they were asked to make. For one thing, the percentage of students admitted to the colleges without even an O-level pass in mathematics or in foreign languages was far too high. Many older women especially, were chary of using the materials and equipment which they were constantly exhorted to try out, preferring to stick to old-fashioned Herbartian methods or, worse, chalk and talk. Young teachers complained that any enthusiasm for the newer methods they had learned in the colleges was quickly stifled in the rigidly structured conditions still prevailing in many schools.

To suggest that the rank and file of primary teachers were incompetent would be insulting, but it has to be said that as a body — through no fault of their own, let it be added — their professionalism left something to be desired. Disruptions caused by chronic wastage among the ranks of newly qualified young women, inability to adapt to new methods by married women returning to service after long years of absence, concurrent courses of training in the colleges which tended to be satisfied with a low level of general education, the rival attraction of careers other than teaching for girl school-leavers, large classes, shortage of staff, pupils who were 'different animals' and more unruly than they used to be, the distractions of T.V., not to mention all those ancillary chores such as meal supervision, guidance and pastoral care which had led to the teacher's role becoming increasingly diffuse — these were some of the causes. No wonder, then, if innovations in the primary school often appeared to be halting and hesitant.

Here, as elsewhere, the rule seems to be that curriculum development is liable to get nowhere unless in the long run it interprets itself as teacher development. But curriculum is not merely a matter of what is taught and how it is taught, it includes the setting in which learning takes place. In this connection the series of Building Bulletins issued by the

Department of Education and Science from 1949 onwards must be reckoned one of the most potent influences in transforming the primary school's way of life. Imaginative and flexible architectural design embodied and made visible theories of primary education which had previously not been easily practicable. Thus Building Bulletin 36 included seven pages of photographs with captions explaining the theoretical principles which the architects had in mind:

1 In primary schools every surface is a work surface, including the floor on which individuals may erect and contrive complex structures.
2 Sizes of working groups vary, and this group of two sought a lobby in which to set up their display and reference material.
3 Frequently all the children come together with their teacher for stories and discussions. Here a space has been improvised by clearing the decks.
4 The dividing line between 'teaching' and 'non-teaching' becomes more distinct as the whole building is drawn into use.
5 The need for small areas for small groups was so great in this primary school that a corner of the assembly hall was screened off to make a reference and private study place.
6 Another example, in which every part of the school is put to full use. Two girls work on problems of calculating areas at one end of the hall, and a larger group do movement at the other.
7 The outside can be used as a valuable extension of the inside if access, visibility and shelter is carefully arranged. This shows one example of how valuable facilities for improvisation and construction can be.

It is unnecessary to point out the contrast between the egg-box structure of the conventional school with its closed cells and its rows of desk-bound pupils in the charge of the same teacher from nine to four o'clock each day and every day, and the openness, freedom of movement and the reliance on pupils as *agents* exemplified by the new design. Given working conditions as spacious and gracious as these, it would be hard for a teacher *not* to adopt a developmental approach even if she or he had never so much as heard of Piaget and was totally unfamiliar with the practice of team-teaching.

Confessing his disillusion with the educational reform movement in the U.S.A. during the 1960s, a movement in which he played a leading part, Bruner is left wondering whether its indifferent success was due to pouring new wine into old bottles. 'A distrust of traditional ways of thinking has brought into question whether schools as such might not be part of the problem — rather than a solution to the problem of education', he wrote. 'Did revision of the curriculum suffice or was a more fundamental restructuring of the entire educational system in order?' And again, 'My work on early education and social class, for example, had convinced me that the educational system was in effect our way of maintaining a class-system — a group at the bottom. It crippled the capacity of children in the lowest socioeconomic quarter of the population to participate at full power in society, and did so early and effectively'[14].

While it would be naive to pretend that England's primary schools have undergone a fundamental restructuring simply because their modernized premises exhibit many of the features associated with 'open' and 'free' schools, there are good grounds for thinking that the face-lift from architectural design has enhanced their morale. At least it has saved them from the internal troubles which beset the reorganization of secondary schools. The best of them are emphatically *not* 'bad places for kids'.

Endorsing the judgement offered at the beginning of this chapter, Stuart Maclure agrees that

Most people would probably say that it has been in the primary schools that the most interesting post-war developments have taken place. It has been here that the continuing tension between 'formal' and 'progressive' ideas has been most clearly seen in practical terms — that is, in actual changes in the way children and teachers spend their time, the things they do, the transactions which take place between them and the environment in which they work.

Many of the ideas and much of the practice go back a long way; much of the theory and the philosophy is fairly shaky, as critics have not hesitated to point out. But, at its pragmatic best, the modern primary school shows more clearly, perhaps, than any other kind of school, the changes in aim and direction in education over the past century, the changed attitude towards children as individual human beings, the contrast in the assumed role of the teacher and the nature of the teacher's authority, the attempt to make schools places where children can freely learn and grow.[15]

Although Maclure was left in no doubt that standards of achievement in the basic subjects had risen consistently during the post-war period, he made the point, which cannot be repeated too often, that these changes related to attitudes and values which cannot be assessed in quantitative terms or set down in a statistical table. Tucked away in its section on costs and priorities, the Plowden Report made the same point:

> The qualities needed in a modern economy extend far beyond skills such as accurate spelling or arithmetic. They include greater curiosity and adaptability, a high level of aspiration, and others which are difficult to measure. To assess these yields from primary education would require long term study of the effects of different systems and different approaches to the education of younger children.[16]

As its title indicated, the report put the interests of the children first. It expressed uneasiness about the existing division of the primary stage into a 5-7 Infants' School and a 7-11 Junior School and recommended an alternative formula for the establishment of a First School (offering a three-year course with one annual September intake at a median age of five years and six months), to be followed by a Middle School (offering a four-year course with a median age range from eight years six months to twelve years six months). It urged the need for a much more generous provision of part-time nursery groups, closer contacts between school and home, improved welfare services and other proposals aimed at equalizing educational opportunity. Of these, the one which aroused most interest, and one of the few to be rigorously implemented, recommended that 'As a matter of national policy, "positive discrimination" should favour schools in neighbourhoods where children are most severely handicapped by home conditions. The programme should be phased to make schools in the most deprived areas as good as the best in the country. For this it may be necessary that their greater claim on resources should be maintained'[17].

The designation of Educational Priority Areas, instigated in the assertive spirit of contemporary ideas about the sociology of knowledge and its distribution, stemmed from the growing concern with the problems posed by rotting inner cities and near-derelict industrial regions. Bruner's fears that the educational system was itself to blame for perpetuating a class system and ensuring that whatever reforms were introduced there was always 'a group at the bottom', seemed to be borne out by the analyses of Bourdieu, Bernstein, Earl Hopper and other leading sociologists. Environmentalism in the up-and-coming social sciences chimed in with the ideology of egalitarianism. For much the same reasons that Marx had decided that previous philosophies had been too content to describe the world whereas the point was to change it, 'interpretative sociology' after 1960 was characterized by its determination to 'do something about it'. The vicissitudes of the massive E.P.A. projects which followed and the relative lack of success which they achieved call for ampler discussion than can be entered into here, but as an attempt to seek remedies for the underprivileged by emphasizing the social contexts of learning these projects clearly moved 'beyond curriculum' in the school-based sense of the term.

But if Plowden is chiefly remembered for the lead given to policies of positive discrimination, the 1967 report was conspicuously lacking in the 'astringent intellectual scrutiny' which it suggested teachers should bring to bear on their day-to-day problems in the classroom. Much of what it had to say about the primary curriculum amounted to little more than a repetition of stale clichés to the effect that 'finding out' is better than 'being told'. Strongly biased by ideas about how children learn in nursery playgroups, it advocated a First School theory and practice which was unashamedly child-centred and, in so doing, left the door open to developments in the Middle School which deserved no better than to be derided as soft-centred. Under the heading of 'Some Practical Implications' for the time-table, it indulged in airy-fairy pronouncements about the 'free day' and the 'integrated curriculum' which, however well-intended, came perilously close to slogan-mongering. Generalizations about flexibility ('Any practice which pre-determines the pattern and imposes it on all is to be condemned') and about 'the boundless curiosity which children have about the world about them', were so flaccid as to leave themselves open to the charge of being complacent, not to say slaphappy. Drawing comfort from the evidence which showed that, despite frequent reports to the contrary, standards of reading ability had been steadily rising since the end of World War II, the report conveniently ignored the fact that the methods adopted by the great majority of primary schools had continued to be of the traditional type. To declare that 'A foreign language, science (as opposed to nature study) and mathematics (as opposed to arithmetic) used to be confined to secondary schools. They are not taught in junior schools. Today there is a basis for a middle school curriculum'[18], raised fears that such a basis would increasingly be drawn into the orbit of secondary schooling. In the event, some fifty L.E.A.s forged ahead with plans for organizing first schools and middle schools, thus making the over-all pattern of English primary education more of a jigsaw than it had been previously.

To make these objections is not to contradict what was said earlier about child-centredness being the leaven which has enlivened and enriched primary education and, indeed, all three stages of the continuous process. But learning does not live by leaven alone. In those schools where the 'free day' and the 'integrated curriculum' were carefully organized *and* where the socioeconomic climate was favourable the results were invariably heartening and often quite admirable. There is everything to be said for allowing pupils to work uninterruptedly to their heart's content without chopping up the time-table into disparate subjects; and since it is clearly impossible for the primary (or any) curriculum to embrace the whole field of human knowledge there is something to be said for an interdisciplinary rationale — and for the view that once adequate norms of attainment in literacy and numeracy have been achieved it really does not matter *what* children learn, even if it means leaving them to their own devices. The question is whether the average child is capable of sustaining his 'boundless curiosity' throughout a 'free day', and whether the informalities of an 'integrated curriculum' may result in a formlessness which is even more boring than a daily routine of 'lessons' and 'subjects'. Even A.S. Neill, after all, was forced to concede that 'Freedom works best with clever children', and Harold Entwistle, whose *Child-centred Education* remains the most balanced review of the pros and cons, makes the caveat that 'It is important to recognize that the integrated curriculum carries as much danger of authoritarianism and miscalculation about the appropriateness of subject matter as does the curriculum based upon distinctive disciplines'[19]. As he remarks wryly, 'It is difficult to conceive of any integrating principle which, by itself, does proper justice to the cultural possibilities of the universe!'[20]

The over-all impression left by Plowden, then, was to condone, while affecting to deplore, the lack of any clear statement of the aims of primary education. 'Phrases such as "whole personality", "happy atmosphere", "full and satisfying life", "full development of powers", "satisfaction of curiosity", "confidence", "perseverance" and "alertness" occurred again and again', it reported.

> This list shows that general statements of aims, even by those engaged in teaching, tend to be little more than expressions of benevolent aspiration which may provide a rough guide to the general climate of a school, but which may have a rather tenuous relationship to the educational practices that actually go on there. ... [adding] It was interesting that some of the headteachers who were considered by H.M. Inspectors to be most successful in practice were least able to formulate their aims clearly and convincingly.[21]

At a time when Bloom's taxonomy was enjoying a vogue and the cult for stating learning objectives in strictly behavioural terms was at its height, this seemingly lax acceptance of the fact that schools reflected the multifarious and conflicting views of a society in flux and that therefore no definition of aims geared to a consensus of opinion, let alone to an orthodoxy, was possible, further exemplified the determination to put the interests of children above all other considerations. Trendy as the Plowden Report may have been in other respects, at least it avoided the trendiness of the programmers who too often forgot that the objective of all the objectives is to ensure that the learner is as strongly motivated at the end of a course as he is at the beginning, preferably more so. Even at its most shiftless, child-centred practice never made *that* mistake. Easy to scoff at 'confidence', 'perseverance' and 'alertness' as expressions of the kind of good intentions which pave the way, if not to Hell, to the slippery slopes of falling academic standards; yet when all is said and done, who can doubt that, by and large, children reaching the age of transfer to secondary schools in Britain in the late 1960s were more self-confident and far less inhibited than were their opposite numbers who were reared under the rigours of the elementary tradition and the shadow of the 11-plus?

Already in 1967, however, reaction against the soft-centred-ness of progressive education had begun to set in. The fulminations of the Black Paper pamphleteers may be seen either as the opening shots in a renewal of the ideological class warfare in the educational history of the Two Nations, or as the onset of a period of 'assertion' (of traditionalism) against the 'domination' (of progressivism) in a Weberian cyclical process which can be observed in educational developments in other countries. What seems to be a seesawing of fashion is no more a matter of chance than are the socioeconomic forces which combine to boost the fortunes of one political party to the point when it becomes strong enough to oust the government of the day. That child-centredness should be favoured during a period of relative affluence is no more surprising than the fact that it suddenly lost favour once the nation's economic crisis became acute. Susan Isaacs, Bertrand Russell and A.S. Neill had always acknowledged that their ideal could only be fully implemented in private schools, in conditions infinitely more auspicious than those

which obtained in the state-maintained system. Any relief from
the duress of the old utilitarian elementary tradition, accordingly, was bound to be at best partial, due as much to changing
methods of child-rearing as to more permissive methods of
teaching in the schools. Any insistence that schools were primarily institutions whose function was to promote individuality and
the freedom for self-expression ran counter to the expectations of
most parents and to the popular view of them as centres devoted
to formal instruction. As Entwistle says, the language of educational debate is often indistinguishable from that of economics:
'education is an *investment*, schools and colleges are *plants*,
graduates are *products* and the salaries of teachers become
subject to *productivity agreements*'[22].

In *A Modern Philosophy of Education*, written in the midst of
the Great Depression, Godfrey Thompson noted that 'In commercial circles a common criticism of the schools has been, for
certainly twenty years and perhaps more, that they no longer
attend to the three R's thoroughly as in the good old days, but
fritter away their time with all sorts of fancy subjects'[23]. Such
criticism might be stilled in the never-had-it-so-good years of the
1950s and 1960s but it was never completely silenced nor refuted
for all its being so ill-founded. Since 1975 it has been pressed
home with renewed vigour, whipped up into a backlash of
opinion which less than a decade ago would have seemed
unthinkably retrograde to most educationists and to most
fair-minded laymen for that matter. This, cynics may reflect
ruefully, is where we came in.

Logic and love in the philosophy of primary education

Language usage, like educational theory, is subject to the whims
of fashion. Following the confrontation with the miners which
brought down the Conservative Government in 1974 the cult
adjective was 'abrasive'. A few years earlier it had been 'astringent', for which, incidentally, *Roget's Thesaurus* offers among
other alternatives 'contracted', 'shrunk', 'strangulated',
'wizened', 'stunted'.

Now if astringent intellectual scrutiny is only made possible by hardening one's heart the inclination will be to decide that children cannot safely be treated as responsible agents and that adults, because of their greater knowledge and maturity, know best what is good for them. Thus, R.S. Peters is led to the conclusion that the interests which really matter are not those which are immediately appealing to the learner but those which are in his long-term interests; and that 'The main function of the teacher is to train and instruct: it is not to help and cure'[24].

Similarly, if the ideas and ideals which endear themselves to the child-centred school of thought are subjected to conceptual analysis many of them can be ridiculed easily enough. In *The Philosophy of Primary Education*, R.F. Dearden enjoyed fair sport in shooting down some of the lame ducks in this field of discourse in which, as he says mockingly, 'All too often what one finds are doctrinal enthusiasms liberally laced with stories about what Sandra or Jonathan, or Sandra did and how deeply satisfying it was'[25]. Considered from a strictly logical point of view, it has to be conceded that many of these doctrines owe more to enthusiasm than to common sense and that some are fallacious. For example, the tendency to equate 'readiness' with 'maturation' fostered the impression that the teacher needed to do nothing but wait and see, leaving the youngster to learn as, when and if the spirit moved him. Certainly, Dearden is within his rights when he asks,

> What is he to teach, if indeed he may 'teach' at all without suffering the pangs of conscience bred in him by an extreme child-centred ideology? Is ignorance in children acceptable so long as good attitudes go along with it? Does arithmetical computation matter any more? Are mis-spelling and mis-shapen handwriting any longer to be a stimulus to correction, or is it enough that the child has 'expressed' himself? Do most things 'just come' if only materials are spread around and everyone is smiled at, continuously?[26]

The question is whether modes of thought which are determined by conceptual analysis alone can preempt the title of *the* philosophy of education, or whether such a philosophy is not itself stunted. Although Hirst and Peters have acknowledged that the main purpose of conceptual analysis is to make explicit the principles underlying the use of words and that *per se* it is not philosophy, they evidently had their tongues in their cheeks when they affirmed that 'Our sympathies are with the progressives in their emphasis on motivational factors in education to which they drew attention with their talk about the needs and interests of children. But our conviction is that this kind of motivation, which is crucial in education, is unintelligible without careful attention to its cognitive core' [27]. The wording here exemplifies the gentle art of damning with faint praise, disparaging in its snide reference to 'talk about the needs and interests of children', unnecessarily hurtful in its suggestion that the progressives' wanton neglect of cognitive learning was 'unintelligible'. Scarcely less unintelligible, surely, was the effect of this obsessional stress on the central importance of cognition in leading to the philosophical judgement that 'We might say that Gandhi or Gaugain were developed human beings because they displayed some human excellence; but they would not necessarily be educated men' [28]. If doctrinal enthusiasm is to be faulted for its occasional absurdities so, it seems, is logical disquisition. Unworthy thought: if professors of philosophy are educated men, are they necessarily developed human beings?

In fact, the interminable discussions about the relationship between freedom and authority, cognition and affectivity, work and play, knowledge and experience, individual and society and, yes, middle-class and working-class attitudes to education, arise from the polarization between a formal philosophy founded on purely rationalistic principles and a less formal one premissed on the kind of human understanding which exists in the mother-child relationship — in a word, on love. One seeks its justification in logical, the other in psychological, explanations. One has recourse to syllogisms, the other to metaphors. The stronger the bias one way or the other the greater becomes the tendency for each side to try to denigrate the other. Thus, those who champion the cause of the 'logic of education' will have no truck with the progressives whom they regard as too tender-minded by half, not to say wishy-washy sentimentalists; while for their part the progressives retort that their opponents' preoccupation with abstract 'forms of knowledge' and 'disciplines', besides being élitist, ultimately reduces education to a desiccated intellectualism.

The antipathies and misunderstandings from this philosophical dualism can be illustrated in a number of ways. Take, for instance, the permanent tension between freedom and authority. So long as this is treated as a problem for conceptual analysis, divorced from any particular existential context, it will be possible to go on playing word games which purport to distinguish between 'freedom from', 'freedom for', 'freedom to', and so on, as if the difference between them somehow depended upon the degree of constraint imposed on each of them. On this reckoning, 'freedom from' can be defined as a negative concept, implying an absence of constraint and hence licence to do as one pleases, therefore a Bad Thing. This, more or less, has been the position taken by thinkers like G.H. Bantock and others who have consistently set their faces against child-centred theory and practice on the grounds that restrictions placed on freedom are necessary since little of value can emerge from the learner's spontaneous interests and self-expression.

By contrast, 'freedom for' and 'freedom to' are held to be positive, presupposing the need for discipline and submission to some external authority. Quite apart from the objection that the apparently logical distinctions drawn between 'positive' and 'negative' freedom are no better than verbal quibbles — as Entwistle points out, 'freedom for' is properly speaking 'freedom from in order to' — any such distinctions disappear in the actual experience of exercising freedom. *Psychologically*, freedom has nothing to do with constraints on choice or impediments to action. Throughout the ages, saints and martyrs have gladly died proclaiming this invincible truth, as have the poets. Logically, it makes no sense at all to say that stone walls do not a prison make, to pretend that a man can count himself king of infinite space though bounded in a nutshell, or that nuns fret not in their narrow rooms. Psychologically, what matters supremely is the conviction, however illusory, of 'being free'. It is this sense of conviction which the child-centred approach seeks to foster and preserve and which traditional practice has tended on the whole to deny. On this issue, needless to say, logic-based and love-based philosophies go their separate ways.

But is it not perverse to maintain that the conviction of 'being free' is worth preserving even if it *is* illusory? Not necessarily. At the very worst it allays the fear of failure which has dogged so many pupils in primary schools in the past. Obviously there are limits placed on any learning situation just as there are walls round prison cells, limits which vary according to individual ability as well as to the demands of the subject matter or skill which has to be mastered. Given brushes and paints and a minimum of priming, any tiny tot takes as easily to child art as he does to child's play. Given a grand piano and the score of Beethoven's 'Emperor' Concerto, he will never be able to play a note unless he is able and willing to receive the necessary tuition and submit to the drudgery of five-finger exercises so that eventually he may acquire the repertoire of keyboard techniques which will enable him to 'express himself'. Superficially, there is a world of difference between these two learning activities. The enabling process common to both, however, consists in the *willingness* to learn. As one of the preconditions for learning any skill, this willingness depends as much upon circumstances as it does upon the level of expertise required for its performance. First among these circumstances is the assurance that 'You can do it'; second, the initial priming by way of example or demonstration by the teacher — 'You do it like this': third, the sense of achievement — 'I can do it and *love* doing it'. The second is the trickiest of the three, especially in the learning of complex skills involving practice over a long period of time, as in learning to play the piano, but provided that the progression from 'I want to' and 'I can' to 'I love to' is sustained, any difficulties encountered are likely to be overcome. In this connection the relevance of Whitehead's stages of Romance, Precision and Generalization, of Bruner's spiral curriculum rising from the enactive to iconic and symbolic levels of conceptualization, and Piaget's Pre-operational, Concrete Operational and Formal Operational stages of intellectual development, seems obvious enough.

It is often said that if children were left to themselves they would never 'pick up' the four rules of arithmetic, no matter how able and willing they happened to be, and this is almost certainly true. What is a good deal less certain is that none of them would ever learn to read in the absence of formal instruction. To repeat, the ability and willingness to learn depend upon circumstances. If a person spends six months in Italy, for example, the probability is that willy-nilly he will 'pick up' enough of the language for normal purposes of communication because circumstances render it imperative for him to do so, whereas if he remains at home the chances are that he will never learn the language despite his being able and willing to do so. Whatever form it takes, the learning experience must be accompanied at all points by the conviction of 'being free' and the sense of 'loving to do it' — the sense which Wordsworth had in mind in confessing that 'T'was pastime to be bound'.

This in turn raises the question of the relationship between work and play. Traditional theory took the view that since adult life was a serious business and the task of earning a living so irksome and full of dreary routine, the sooner children were brought to face the harsh realities of the world outside the school walls, the better for them. The morality of an industrialized Protestant ethic decreed that a man must fulfil himself through work, and that any spare time left over from his labours should be used for recuperative purposes or else be construed as idleness. Now that job satisfaction counts for more than it did fifty years ago, this guilt complex attaching to play has largely been dissipated, but enough of it remains to keep alive suspicions that schools which adopt a developmental approach 'fritter away their time with all sorts of fancy subjects'. While no one is prepared to say outright, 'Do let's be beastly to the children', many parents and teachers are privately of the opinion that forcing pupils to learn things which are of no immediate interest to them does no great harm, even if it goes against the grain. Licking them into shape, it used to be called.

In general, this remains the standpoint of a logic-based philosophy of primary education. Dearden takes exception to the concept of play because of the immense variety of its manifestations. The child's play, he says, is 'non-serious' in the sense that it has no ethical value. (Really? — as if his whole vocation were endless imitation?) 'What we play at is intrinsically unimportant. It can therefore be easily seen why people should so often have said that play is "free" for indeed it is: it is free from the demands of the serious. We do not *neglect* our play, as we may neglect our moral obligations, or neglect to treat fundamental values with proper seriousness' [29].

Again, 'Play is *self-contained*, and this is our second proposition about it. It is self-contained in the sense that it is set apart from the duties, deliberations and developing projects which make up the serious web of purposes of ordinary life' [30].

How seriously is the high serious tenor of this kind of reasoning to be taken? If it comes to a choice between Dearden's gruff declaration that 'Caldwell Cook was just wrong in thinking a child's interest to be all in play', and Rousseau's axiom that child's play is *opus*, a wholehearted affair which all too easily becomes wearisome as *labor* under the heavy-handed interference of adults, how does the vote go? On this score, a love-based philosophy has never been in any doubt. If job satisfaction is a desideratum in the adult world or work, the satisfaction derived from play activities is a *sine qua non* for the young child's nurture. Through them he learns intuitively the need for rules, for self-restraint, for cooperation, for obligations which are freely engaged in because freely accepted. It is not simply that, as a child, he is blithely unaware of any difference between work and play: regardless of age, the good life admits of no hard and fast distinction between the two.

> Pursuits which are highly esteemed in civilized communities — theatre and concert-going, reading poetry, making music and dance, painting and looking at pictures, for example, have the distinguishing features of play. Thus, whilst most of our activity in the market place is instrumental in character, there exists for most men (and increasingly so in highly industrialized communities) a play life whose main characteristic is that it is an area of life in which we can exercise considerable choice of activity. Moreover, much of what we do

in this area of life is not vital, since it is a matter of indifference biologically whether we read novels, listen to music, or play Bingo in preference to either of these things .... With the growth of leisure, an increasing proportion of living will be a play life in this sense.[31]

Next, the motivational differences affecting middle-class and working-class attitudes to education. It was suggested earlier that changes in patterns of child-rearing in an increasingly permissive society had had more to do with bringing about a relaxation of the formal regimen in primary schools than all the child-centred theories put together. This seems to be borne out by research findings in Britain and the U.S.A. which show fairly consistently that, regardless of class, over-achievers tend to come from families classified as affectionate, whereas under-achievers tend to come from families in which parental relationships are authoritarian. All the evidence indicates that children exposed to restrictive discipline, not least that of a domineering father-figure, are more conforming and more dependent than children brought up in more permissive families.

All of these studies imply a linear relationship between parental authority and achievement; that is to say, that the more or less authoritarian the parent the greater or less the level of achievement.... A number of studies have been carried out to determine which methods seem to be the most effective in securing conformity from the children to parental expectations and, although these studies use different measures, there is a common core of agreement that the use of approval or disapproval as disciplinary techniques and the use of reasoning and explanation, are conducive to the development of conscience. The use of coercive methods of discipline, on the other hand, including the use of physical punishment, appear to result in a moral orientation based on the fear of authority. The explanation which is advanced for the effectiveness of love-oriented methods of handling children is that children internalize parental expectations as a means of retaining parental warmth and protection. Consequently, the internalization process tends to be most successful in a family environment where there is frequent and warm interaction between parent and child, but where training and discipline evoke a fear of the loss of love.[32]

Earlier marriages, longer life expectation, immigration, working mothers, unmarried mothers, pre-marital and extra-marital sex, slum clearance, new housing schemes, mortgages rates, divorce rates, legalized abortion — these are only some of the factors which have brought about major changes in family life. Add to these the phenomenon referred to by physiologists as the secular trend towards earlier physical maturity, the steady lowering of the age of puberty and all the behavioural side-effects which attend it, and the complexities of Britain's recent social history are only too apparent. Beyond saying that there has been an all-round loosening of ties in the structure of the family and that this has been conducive to greater informality in institutional schooling, it is wiser to refrain from generalizations.

Although it is known that home background is a more potent educational influence than schooling, the reasons why the will to succeed is strong in some children and weak or absent in others are as yet imperfectly understood. If the notion of innate intelligence has been shown to be false, no less false has been the view of motivation as an inner drive popularized by child-centred theorists. This is not to deny the existence of natural impulses, merely to recognize that the extent to which their potential is realized depends upon environmental stimuli — in a word, on nurture.

Early studies indicated that such variables as weaning, baby-feeding and early toilet-training accounted for differences in the formation of working-class and middle-class personalities and cognitive styles. Family size, too, was the subject of several investigations which revealed an inverse correlation between the number of siblings and scores in verbal reasoning tests. Latterly the focus of attention has switched from the family to the subculture, in particular to sociolinguistic research. In a field which is constantly shifting its ground and in which hypothesis rather than proof is the order of the day any attempt to summarize the evidence would be premature. The gist of it is given in Bernstein's oft-quoted imaginary conversations between a middle-class mother and child and a working-class mother and child on a bus. When the bus is about to move off, the first says, 'Hold tight, darling', then patiently answers the child's questions, gives reasons, offers explanations and enters into a dialogue. The other does not: any two-way verbal communication is cut short by the command, 'Shut up and do as I tell you'. As a vignette of love-oriented vis-à-vis authoritarian methods of child-rearing, the picture given reflects the same contrast which is to be found between progressive and traditional methods of teaching in the schools.

While Bernstein's hypothetical 'elaborated' and 'restricted' language codes have subsequently been modified — in their original form they were widely misrepresented — there is no doubt that linguistic difficulties account in a large measure for poor motivation and low levels of aspiration. The sense of discontinuity between the language codes of home and school is, for many, also a sense of discontinuity in cultural and value codes. Says Lawton:

> Sociologists are becoming increasingly interested in the fact that the difficulty of working-class children adjusting to school is a problem of discontinuity — they come to school with attitudes, and expectations (acquired in the process of being socialized into a working-class sub-culture) which are very different from the middle-class culture of the school. This is a problem in itself, but it poses very difficult questions relating to the problems of code learning. If Bernstein's view of context, role, culture and language is accepted, then code learning, or extending pupils' range of control over language, must be achieved through changes in the social structure of the school, through extended possibilities in developing new role-relations.[33]

As to that, the inference must be that if apathy, passive resistance and open rebellion are nothing like so rife among 5-11-year-olds as they are among adolescents it is because the social structure of primary schools has been 'broadened and humanized' to an extent far beyond anything the Hadow Committee dreamed of in 1931. Broadened in the sense that its range of learning activities is wider and more in keeping with the stages of mental, emotional and physical development of children; humanized in being as responsive to the demands of love as it is to the dictates of logic.

The debate about standards

There the account might well have been closed. If not entirely impartial in its appraisal, the account might have been reckoned faithful enough in recording developments which established the principle that the primary stage exists in its own right, not simply as a preparation for secondary education. Until 1976, that is. Suddenly the climate of opinion turned decidedly chilly. Within months much of the goodwill enjoyed by the progressives during the previous decade was withdrawn. With rampant inflation and rising unemployment in everyone's minds, the pressure on the schools to serve utilitarian, economic purposes was renewed. Significantly, Dr Bennett's team survey of the effects of traditional, mixed and progressive teaching styles in north-west England was publicized by the news media in highly sensational terms. Its findings, equivocal as they were, were immediately seized on by intemperate right-wing critics and adduced as proof that formal methods were best after all and that it was time to put a stop to all this activity and experience nonsense. A more impartial assessment of the research evidence might have been that it confirmed what was already known, i.e. that formal instruction gets 'results' in formal subjects like arithmetic, grammar or spelling, but that informal methods are more appropriate and more effective in the humanities and sciences where learning skills cannot be acquired through drill alone — and that there is a place for both.

The 1976 mood, however, was less than impartial. All the lurking fears and suspicions which had been simmering during years of continuing change came to a head, nowhere more hysterically than in the William Tyndale primary school where staff, parents, managers and local authority inspectors found themselves so completely at loggerheads that the dispute could only be resolved by ordering a public enquiry. The notoriety attending that undignified brawl, from which none of the parties concerned emerged entirely unscathed, sent its own shock waves across a worried nation. If this kind of anarchical situation could arise in one school, what was there to prevent it in others, it was asked? Should not teachers be made more accountable for achieving satisfactory standards in the basic subjects? Had teachers been given too free a hand? Was it not true that the teaching of reading had been grossly neglected?

It was not true. All the available research evidence upheld the conclusion that at least until 1975 there was no justification for the belief that reading standards were declining, but presumably this evidence was not newsworthy it was conveniently ignored. What *was* true was that a substantial proportion of non-readers and poor readers still existed. No prizes for guessing who these unfortunates were, where they were to be found, or by what their failure was caused. This 'group at the bottom' was mainly comprised of children from poor homes, concentrated in decayed city centres, attending schools in which rapid turnover of staff ruled out any possibility of consistency in the methods of teaching reading or any other subjects. For young, inexperienced teachers caught between the claims and counter-claims of i.t.a. (initial teaching alphabet), 'look and say', 'phonic methods', flash cards and the rest, constant chopping and changing was bewildering enough, still more so for their pupils. For children whose parents were among the two million functional illiterates in the adult population (scarcely a good advertisement for traditional methods) it was nothing less than disastrous. It is not entirely sardonic to suggest that most children learn to read not so much because of the efficacy of this or that method of teaching as despite it. For those who lack any vestige of the will to succeed this is not the case: they are turned off from the start.

Public concern about falling standards, however, has not centred on this 'group at the bottom'; on the contrary, it has been voiced chiefly by middle-class people, the very ones whose interests the schools are alleged to favour. The current debate would be more honest and meaningful if it were less bemused by *standards* and more concerned with *criteria*.

In the first place, *standards* tend to be conceived of very loosely, capable of meaning whatever pedagogical folklore chooses them to mean. In the second, *standards* are invariably retrospective in the sense that they refer to levels of achievement attained in the past. This leads employers, for example, to complain that recruitment is increasingly difficult because young applicants for jobs can no longer write a decent letter or do simple mathematical calculations, unmindful of the fact that many of the school-leavers on whom they formerly drew are now to be found in full-time further or higher education. The mistake of ah-the-past evaluation is to compare like with unlike.

In the technical jargon of educational assessment, *standards* may either be 'criterion-referenced' or 'norm-referenced'. In the first, a pupil is judged by whether or not he has scraped past an absolute, fixed limit on a scale of achievement; in the second, by his relative position on the scale, i.e. by comparing the pupil's individual performance with the distribution of achievements in the relevant pupil population. There is little point, therefore, in making comparisons over time without taking into account differences in aims resulting from the broadening and humanizing developments which have taken place in primary education since 1944. It may, of course, be argued that in attempting to do too much the primary schools have dissipated their efforts; instead of doing one job really efficiently, as in the days of the old elementary school, they now serve a variety of functions and excel in none. It may be that we have been led to expect far too much of teachers, pupils and schools, and that the accusation of falling standards merely reflects the rise in levels of expectation. Should we cut our losses and settle for what Bereiter thinks is the only honest solution, i.e. concentrate on the two objectives which the primary school *can* achieve — training in the basic skills and the provision of custodial care? Is it fraudulent to keep up the pretence that anything more, or better, can be offered? Would not a primary-school staff consisting of three Rs specialist instructors and child-care aides represent a more rational division of labour than the one we have?

Certainly there is something to be said for establishing national norms of achievement in basic literacy and numeracy, although those who advocate this gloss over the fact that it is easier said than done. Such a move, one imagines, would be welcomed by the great majority of all-purpose teachers if only because it set tangible targets for formal instruction and, in so doing, enabled them to concentrate on tasks which they regard as more important. If, for example, the morning sessions were devoted exclusively to the three Rs and the afternoons left free for informal activities — as happened under the Winnetka plan — might not the resulting compromise prove equally satisfactory to both traditional and radical opinion?

Until a few years ago it rarely occurred to anyone except philosophers of education to ask what schools were *for*. The fact that it has become fashionable to do so is itself the measure of uncertainty in our frames of reference. This uncertainty is reflected in the confusion of values inculcated in the schools, simultaneously emphasizing the need for individual competition and the need for social cooperation. What is missing in the schools, as in the national life, is any sense of dedication to a supreme cause. G.H. Bantock's comment is more pertinent today than it was when he made it in 1952:

> It seems to me that the most pressing problem of the moment in education — as in the whole of our social life — is the search for an 'authority' that will give strength and meaning to man's free development of himself, that will allow man to come to his true 'self', in Lawrence's significance of the term — which in the last resort is what education implies. That authority cannot be found within the circle of the self, nor can it be found in terms of other selves only.[34]

In the past the categorical imperatives supplied by religion and patriotism made it unnecessary to ask what schools were for. Instead of worrying about the possibility of declining standards in reading, writing and arithmetic, the current debate might be conducted more responsibly than it has been so far if it paid more attention to the causes underlying the manifest decline in religious observance and religious belief in any shape or form. If the philosophy of primary education is to be governed by logic we know what the outcome will be in a pluralistic society: 'First of all, religious instruction, prayer and worship would disappear, though there would be incidental teaching about religion, in literature, history and social studies, for example'[35].

For all its sins of omission and commission, a child-centred developmental approach may therefore be seen as the last, best hope of kindling any residual sparks of spirituality in the young. But for it, the drift towards secular humanism would have been irresistible and the way left open for the further prostitution of education in the name of saleable skills. If all is not well in the state of the nation or in other sectors of its education system, it seems good advice to 'leave well alone' so far as our primary schools are concerned.

Postscript

Since the demise of the last of the 'Great Educators', John Dewey, educational thought has been the province of small fry and the commanding heights of policy-making occupied by a race of little men. In any review of developments at the primary stage, reference has to be made to the influence of psychologists like Piaget and Bruner but it would be hard to name a single British worker in the field with a comparable international reputation. The exception was, of course, an odd-man-out, a lonesome prophet without honour in his own country, yet one who deserves the passing tribute of a sigh.

'Death for me means never knowing whether freedom will prevail', he wrote with typical humour and resignation during his last illness. 'If on the Washington-Moscow analogy there comes a hot line from Hell give me a ring and let me know how things progress.

Yours,

Neill.'

References ·

1 *Education in 1938* (Board of Education Annual Reports), p.41.
2 W. Boyd and W. Rawson, *The Story of the New Education* (Heinemann, 1965), p.39.
3 D.E.M. Gardner, *Susan Isaacs: the First Biography* (Methuen, 1969), pp.61-2.
4 A. Clegg, *The Changing Primary School* (Chatto, 1972), p.8.
5 Report of the Consultative Committee of the Board of Education, *The Primary School* (H.M.S.O., 1931), introduction.
6 W.K. Richmond, *Purpose in the Junior School* (Redman, 1949), pp.208-9.
7 Clegg, op. cit., p.51.
8 R.J.W. Sellick, *The New Education* (Pitman, 1968), p.213.
9 Clegg, op. cit., p.175.
10 J. Blackie, *Good Enough for the Children?* (Faber, 1963), p.16.
11 K. Mannheim and W.A.C. Stewart, *Introduction to the Sociology of Education* (Routledge, 1962), p.136.
12 P.E. Vernon, 'The bearing of recent advances in psychology on educational problems', *Studies in Education* (University of London Institute of Education), no. 7.
13 W.A.L. Blyth, *English Primary Education: a Sociological Description* (Routledge, 1965), vol. 1, p.81.
14 J.S. Bruner, *The Relevance of Education* (Allen & Unwin, 1972), pp.x-xi.
15 S. Maclure, *One Hundred Years of London Education* (Allen Lane, 1970), p.156.
16 Report of the Central Advisory Council for Education (England), *Children and their Primary Schools* (H.M.S.O., 1967), vol. I, para. 1175.
17 ibid., Recommendations and Conclusions, para. 8.
18 ibid, para. 371.
19 H. Entwistle, *Child-centred Education* (Methuen, 1970), p.116.
20 ibid., p.107.

have been forgiven for saying, 'A plague o' both your houses'.
As the Assistant Masters' Association noted:

> This tension, which has increased ever since 1944, is between
> two opposed but equally dangerous theories, either of which
> finds few sponsors among English educationists. On the one
> hand the segregation of the intellectually most gifted children
> to their detriment and that of others … on the other hand,
> equally harmful is the indiscriminate herding together of
> children of very varying ability, as in the non-selective
> American Comprehensive high schools. [3]

For the most part, graduate teachers fought shy of any schemes
for the merging of grammar and modern schools; in their
considered opinion any attempt to do so was as foolish as trying
to mix oil and water. The National Union of Teachers, the most
powerful professional association and the one with a majority of
non-graduate members, remained uncommitted. This wait-and-
see attitude, thinks Manzer, 'was particularly necessary because,
in addition to external party divisions, the membership was
internally divided on the desirability of reorganization' [4].

All this, be it remembered, was in the days when rank-and-
file opinion rationalized its uncertainties by pretending that it
was possible to 'keep politics out of education'. All the same,
like it or lump it, the debate about 'going comprehensive'
needed to be placed fairly and squarely in its ideological context.
Throughout the 1950s it could be said that anything resembling
an agreed national policy for secondary education was nowhere
in sight. It was not simply that most L.E.A.s were already
committed to making separatist arrangements and that changing
course in midstream was out of the question — although the
near-impossibility of imposing any semblance of a uniform
pattern on the patchwork quilt of 146 different plans has to be
recognized. The fact that, in general, Labour-controlled L.E.A.s
were determined to hang on to their grammar schools whereas
West Wales (a Liberal stronghold) and Westmorland (held by
the Conservatives) were among the first areas to go comprehensive suggests that the real constraints on local planning were
demographic and economic rather than ideological. For a long

time it seemed as though the discussions raging over the alleged evils of the 11-plus examination, streaming and social-class inequalities were fated to get nowhere, a safety valve for those who were full of passionate intensity, possibly, otherwise merely shadow-boxing and hot air. With the Ayes cancelled out by the Noes, the outcome at least temporarily was a stalemate. In a stop-go decade, 'going comprehensive' resembled a game of musical chairs.

Did all this exemplify the English genius for muddling through or was it symptomatic of that vacillating frame of mind which foreigners have diagnosed as the English Disease? Hard to say, harder still to decide which of the pressure groups engaged in the power struggle would emerge as the main trend-setter. At this point, therefore, it may be convenient to break off and consider some of the causes underlying the apparent impasse. Having done that, the next step will be to examine the course of development in grammar, technical and modern schools. It should then be easier to see just how and why ideological and pragmatic trends have gradually converged in broadly the same direction, adding momentum to the drive towards a consensus in favour of a phased reorganization of secondary education on comprehensive lines.

The question of social justice

In order to understand the controversies surrounding the comprehensive school, it is advisable to take some account of three competing theories which have played their part in twentieth-century discussions of the problem of social justice. On the understanding that the labels assigned to them here are not to be taken as in any way indicative of party-political affiliations, these theories may be summarized as follows:

(1) *Conservative theory* sees society as a hierarchy of functionally related classes. Classes are not to be thought of as divisive, but valued because they provide the cement which enables society to cohere. T.S. Eliot's *Notes towards a Definition of Culture* is a typical modern statement of this point of view, which has an intellectually respectable lineage dating back to

Ancient Greece. Individual roles and status are held to be to a great extent biologically and historically determined — which explains a preference for psychologists like Burt, Jensen and Eysenck. Since ability and class position are closely correlated, there is little or no room for upward or downward mobility. 'Sponsored mobility', therefore, is perfectly legitimate in a natural aristocracy of talent. Normally, then Conservative theory is satisfied which the *status quo*: old-established institutions, it insists, must not be tampered with unless it is absolutely necessary.

(2) *Liberal theory*, likewise, agrees that individual abilities are extremely variable. It accepts inequality as inevitable but is against inherited privilege. Accordingly, Liberal theory stresses the need for greater equality of opportunity in education. Access to education should not be made easier for one class to the detriment of others. 'Contest mobility' is essential for the promotion of a genuine meritocracy. On the whole, Liberal theory is dissatisfied with the *status quo* but is confident that a new order can be brought about by means of 'rolling' reforms.

(3) *Socialist theory* is uncompromisingly egalitarian. It maintains that observed differences in individual ability and status are almost entirely determined by environmental influences, in particular the economic system and the division of labour in industrial (capitalistic) society. Socialist theory is contemptuous of traditional institutions and values which it sees as exploitative, fraudulent and corrupt. It is impatient with what it regards as ineffectual liberal reforms and demands nothing less than a total restructuring of society.

In both Conservative and Liberal theory, social justice means investing power and authority in those who are best fitted to rule, i.e. either a natural élite wedded to a policy of No Change or a meritocratic élite dedicated to a policy of gradual change. By comparison, Socialist theory is more revolutionary in urging the claims of participatory democracy and the rights of individuals to make their own decisions.

Historically, Conservative theory may be said to have dominated policy-making in education from the Middle Ages until the beginning of the nineteenth century. In its 'pure' form it is now defunct, although sufficient traces of it remain to influence die-hard opinion. Liberal theory inspired most of the social reforms from 1832 to the present day. In its 'pure' form it is no longer in the ascendant, however. While its tenets remain by far the most popular of the three theories, the apparent failure of successive reforms to remove social inequalities has led to their validity being questioned, not least by the rising generation. The onset of Socialist theory is quite recent: as one reviewer puts it, 'The Marxism of Marxism has barely begun'[5].

If Conservative theory represents a flat denial of equality of opportunity and Liberal theory promises only equality of opportunity to be unequal, Socialist theory is not to be satisfied with anything less than equality of achievement. Implications of its 'strong programme in the sociology of knowledge' are as yet too far-reaching and too drastic for the theory to command widespread acceptance in the educational field, where inertia and vested interests combine to ensure the maintenance of the established system. Nevertheless, that system has found it politic in recent years to make concessions to the increasingly aggressive thrust of egalitarianism. Anthony Crosland's 'strong' definition of equality of opportunity provides one example of this, Plowden's 'positive discrimination' another. The 'warming-up' process which has brought rising levels of expectation and aspiration in its train and resulted in Britain's becoming much more nearly a classless society than it was before the Second World War, suggests that this third type of theory is destined to prevail in future. Socialist theory heralds the long delayed advent of the Age of the Common Man as it used to be called.

At any rate, few people nowadays would care or dare to dissent from the view that 'Common schools are meaningless unless they transmit a common culture and provide an adequate means for *individual development* within the general framework of that culture'[6]. Against this,

Despite the fact that we have officially moved away from a 'two nations' view of education and society the present system of education continues to give upper and middle class children access to preferential occupational placement (as has been documented by sociologists), but the education system continues to socialise the children of the upper strata into élite values and élite ways of thinking — the reality system of the ruling class. Conversely, working class pupils are frequently *kept* different by the education system, despite its ideals of equality (Only a few are deliberately sponsored and resocialised into values of the sponsoring group); this is made easier by the fact that the working class can be seen by teachers as a group with a view of reality different from the view of reality of the educators. [7]

It hardly needs to be said that the dynamic of the common-school ideal stems from forces *outside* the education system. These forces are primarily demographic, economic and technological and only secondarily social and political. (The strength of Socialist theory, incidentally, resides in its all-out emphasis on environmental factors.) Thus the growing pressure of demand, not simply for free secondary education for all but for upper secondary and higher education, reflects the growing demands of a consumer society for better-paid jobs and higher standards of living, demands which are in turn only to be satisfied by the creation of an ever-widening range of skilled manpower.

In general, the education systems of Western European countries have been slower to respond to these forces than the U.S.A. Chronologically, Sweden was the first of them to adopt a concerted system approach which resulted in an all-through reorganization being accomplished in the 1950s and 1960s. By comparison, West Germany has been much slower in getting off the starting line. Progress in France and Britain may be thought to be midway between that of Sweden and West Germany. Without going so far as to say that each national system is *sui generis* it is evident that each has its peculiar problems and its own way of dealing with them. At the same time, comparative studies reveal a worldwide trend towards the common-school principle. Variations in the rate of progress in implementing it, can be accounted for to some extent by the interplay of the three above theories, depending upon which of them is predominant in the climate of opinion and policy-making.

This being so, it is instructive to see what has happened in the New World. The American high school became fully comprehensive after 1890 when the Committee of Ten sought in vain to restrict it to college preparatory courses of the grammar-school type. Until that time most American academics and administrators had shared Thomas Jefferson's conviction that 'We must rake the genius from the rubbish annually' — an expression of Liberal theory with Conservative overtones. The opposing view represented by Andrew Jackson was anti-élitist, even anti-intellectual, but more in keeping with the spirit of the melting pot of nations *and* its Constitution, and to that extent the one which, if only by sheer force of numbers, recommended itself to grassroots opinion. To this day, American education is affected by this uneasy tension between Jacksonian and Jeffersonian philosophies — a reminder that the inherent conflict between Conservative-Liberal and Socialist outlooks has only been partially resolved even in a nation professing the faith that 'all men are created equal'. If only because the U.S.A. was the first democracy to go comprehensive, the vicissitudes of the American high school are worth noting, for it seems certain that they will be paralleled, if not exactly repeated, in Britain and other countries.

Developments in the schools

The secondary modern school From its genesis in *The Education of the Adolescent,* the secondary modern school was designed to 'provide a good all-round secondary education, not focused primarily on the traditional subjects of the school curriculum, but *developing out of the interests of the children'*. In the flowery rhetoric of Hadow, it was to do this 'through the placing of youth, in the hour of its growth, "as it were in the fair meadow" of a congenial and inspiring environment'. A child-centred approach was deemed appropriate for the mass of pupils who had neither the ability nor the aptitude for a full-length academic course, and despite Hadow's recommendation to the contrary it was decided that the modern school should be free from the pressure of external examinations. Any suggestion of its aping the grammar school was to be avoided. Activity and experience, projects and centres of interest were to provide the pabulum for a 'good all-round secondary education', with any vocational bias deferred until the later stages of the course. In this way, it was hoped, the modern school would evolve its own distinctive life-style and justify itself as an attractive and worthwhile alternative to the grammar school.

The Newsom Report, wistfully entitled *Half Our Future* (1963), still clung to this fond hope but while acknowledging that here and there there had been 'some splendid achievements in the schools', concluded that

> the future pattern of employment in this country will require a much larger pool of talent than is at present available; and that at least a substantial proportion of the 'average' and 'below average' pupils are sufficiently educable to supply that additional talent. The need is not only for more skilled workers to fill existing jobs, but also for a generally educated and intelligently adaptable labour force to meet new demands.[8]

In reaching this conclusion the report was strongly influenced by the growing evidence of widespread social deprivation, set out in detail in its statistical tables and more graphically in its profiles of the Brown, Jones and Robinson children. It revealed that nearly eighty per cent of modern-school buildings were seriously deficient, that the qualifications of modern-school teachers were often as 'below average' as their pupils were said to be, that rapid turnover of staff vitiated the work of schools in the poorer districts — in short that more than half the nation's children were getting a raw deal. Besides reiterating the case for raising the leaving age without further delay, it urged the need for more intellectually demanding courses to counteract the aimless drift and low morale which characterized the work of many schools, particularly among older pupils.

In sum, the Newsom message amounted to saying that the abilities of the broad mass of children had been grossly underestimated and that, given the chance, they were capable of better things. In a memorable passage in his preface to the report, Sir Edward Boyle, Conservative Minister of Education at the time, was bold enough to affirm that 'Intelligence as measured by the tests so far applied is largely an acquired characteristic.'

Clearly, the 'Newsom children', as they came to be called, were a mixed bunch. At one end of the ability range there were those who, but for the luck of the draw, might have found a place in grammar school; at the other, those who came near to being classified as educationally subnormal. For the higher-ability groups the lack of any incentive in the shape of a leaving certificate tended to be frustrating. Turned loose in the 'fair meadow', there was nowhere for them to go. For the rest, what was supposed to be a 'congenial and inspiring environment' was often little better than the bleak regimen of the old senior elementary school.

These and other deficiencies were recognized but, as Maclure pointed out,

> The report is notable for the absence of any assessment of the merits of different forms of organization for secondary education. The Council took the view that secondary modern schools and, even more so, comprehensive schools had not been in existence long enough for any valid judgments to be made about which was better, and preferred to tackle the problem on the assumption that the educational needs of these children would be the same irrespective of the type of school organization adopted. They were encouraged to this *pis aller* by the fact that the questionnaires used to collect the information tabulated in their survey were not constructed so as to give any guidance on the question of organization; and that a unanimous report was facilitated by evading this contentious issue.[9]

Could it be that the Council's terms of reference were deliberately framed so as to exclude any possibility of the modern school poaching on the grammar school's preserves? During the 1950s there had been a growing tendency for modern-school pupils to stay on voluntarily beyond the leaving age — from 9,000 in 1949, the numbers doing so had risen to 21,000 in

1957 — and many of these became candidates for the General Certificate of Education examination at the O-level. In 1954 secondary modern schools presented 5,500 candidates — ten times that number in 1964. In 1958 a Conservative Party White Paper, *Secondary Education for All — a New Drive*, encouraged them to develop post-O-level courses, blithely unmindful of the fact that the prospects for doing so successfully were slim to the point of being negligible. Nevertheless, this eager vying for paper qualifications was a new departure and one which, if not entirely unexpected, ran counter to the original concepts and assumptions of tripartitism.

Following the Beloe Report, then, the Minister announced in 1963 that a new type of external examination for a Certificate of Secondary Education (C.S.E.) was to be introduced. As a test of proficiency for fifth-year pupils in a wide range of subjects, it was to be awarded in Grades from 1 to 5. Grade 1 was to be considered equivalent to an O-level G.C.E. pass, the lower grades correspondingly less difficult so as to offer pupils of average and below-average ability reasonable chances of succeeding. In order to obtain a certificate, at least one Grade 4 pass in one subject was to be required, otherwise there was no question of anyone failing the examination. In addition, under Mode 3 regulations, schools were to be allowed to design their own courses and assess them internally. Like the G.C.E., the C.S.E. was to be administered by Regional Boards.

At the time, many feared that the new certificate would inevitably turn out to be a very second-best affair, a worthless piece of paper in the eyes of employers. In some areas — London, Bristol, Lancashire and Cheshire — regional examinations of the Beloe type has been in existence for several years, but for the great majority of modern-school pupils it had so far been a case of Hobson's choice — G.C.E. or nothing. Not surprisingly, then, as examinations go, the C.S.E. was an instantaneous success. At long last, even the humblest dwellers in the 'fair garden' had tangible incentives to work for. Professional morale, too, was enhanced. In anticipation of the raising of the leaving age, more and more teachers became actively engaged in the preparation of courses, in testing and evaluation. In particular, the experience gained through the monitoring and continuous assessment of Mode 3 schemes of work proved to be invaluable. Under the aegis of the Schools Council (established in 1964), the curriculum development movement entered its heyday in a mood of mild euphoria. Nuffield-sponsored projects and most of the multifarious local and regional pilot projects centred directly or indirectly on the problems of improving the quality of education for the 'Newsom children'. Teachers' Centres sprang up like daisies up and down the country — workshops for the design of new courses and the testing and production of learning materials. Resource Centres began to appear. So did the Certificate of Extended Education (C.E.E.), intended for 17-year-olds whose scholastic attainments fell short of G.C.E. A-levels and inaugurated on an experimental basis only.

Praiseworthy and imaginative as many of these initiatives undoubtedly were, all were marked by the tacit assumption that there was an irreducible distinction between academic and non-academic learning and teaching. Programmed learning, audio-visual aids, or a box of tricks handed over from one or other of the curriculum development projects, might be all very well for modern-school pupils who had nothing better to do, certainly not for those in grammar schools, where the emphasis remained firmly on exacting scholarship and the formal disciplines. The over-all effect was to perpetuate the 'separate but equal' illusion. 'With one or two exceptions', says Holly, 'they assume the *status quo*, including the divided system ... ', an opinion which he backs by quoting John White's castigation of the early Working Papers issued by the Schools Council: 'Instead of pressing for a common curriculum for all pupils, for a common depth in the disciplines to which all pupils should be expected to have penetrated, they give us a streamline curriculum in the elementary school tradition' [10].

M.F.D. Young agrees. So long as high-status knowledge is associated with the values of dominant groups in society, maximum resistance to any innovations in academic curricula must be expected.

This is supported by evidence from the work of the Schools

Council. The Council has accepted the stratification of knowledge and produces most of its recommendations for reform in
the low-status knowledge areas. These tend to be associated
with curricula which are for younger and less able children and
are not linked to the interests of those who are in positions of
power in the social structure![11]

In the meantime, the numbers of modern-school pupils entered
for both G.C.E. and C.S.E. continued to increase by leaps and
bounds. Since the G.C.E. O-level overlapped with C.S.E. Grade
1, the borderline between the two examinations had become a
good deal hazier than it had been in the days when the former
was reserved exclusively for grammar-school candidates. Granted, the latter were usually expected to aim for at least five
'good' O-levels whereas the aims of all but the very best
modern-school pupils tended to be less ambitious, so that there
was a sizeable gap between the two group performances. For the
first time, however, it became possible to query the necessity for
separate examinations. Changes in the sociology of knowledge,
moreover, made it possible to query the supremacy of academic
awards and to give more credit for Mode 3-type courses conducted on 'activity and experience' lines.

According to H.C. Dent, 'The twenty years following 1945
saw in the Secondary Modern school a process of evolution
unmatched for speed and significance in the history of English
education ... . But the full story remains to be told; when it is, it
will prove to be as exciting and encouraging a story as any to be
found in the annals of education'[12]. High praise. Many
educationists of Dent's generation would doubtless have agreed
that it was well merited. In their estimation, the modern school
had seized its opportunities and more than justified the hopes
placed in it back in 1926: it had made good.

But William Taylor's appraisal of developments was decidedly
less sanguine:

The attempt to establish a new concept of secondary education for the bulk of the population, untrammelled by the
demands of the school certificate or other examinations
designed chiefly for university entrance, has met with

:onspicuous failure. In fact, those schools which, by their emphasis on activity and experience rather than formal subject methods, have tried to carve out for themselves a new path for adolescent education are now obliged to fight a rearguard action against the questioning of their standards of attainment, pressure from parents to provide examination courses, and the difficulties of being 'odd school out' in the local area. The attempt to create a *distinctive* type of modern school education was foredoomed to failure because of its inherent contradictions. It was at one and the same time a vehicle for the integrative idealism of the left and the exclusive separation of the right.

And again,

In rejecting the role that was cast for it in 1944, the Modern school has on the one hand been rejecting much that was new in the field of secondary education, and on the other asserting its right to compete with other types of school in the only terms that society recognises for the ascription of status. It may be that the Modern school is neither staffed nor equipped to undertake academic and technical work, and that such work is performed less effectively and with poorer results than by a grammar or technical school working with the same pupils. The very fact of the attempts being made, however, serves to diminish the status distinctions between the different types of secondary school, to reduce parental anxiety regarding the outcome of the eleven-plus examination, and to divert attention from the consideration of whether a complete restructuring of secondary education is necessary .... Now that the work of grammar, technical and modern schools is tending to converge in terms of pragmatic, rather than theoretical, conceptions of what secondary education should involve, there is even less justification than before for the educational and social inequalities of the tripartite system.[13]

A melancholy conclusion. After 1963, albeit reluctantly, it gradually came to be shared by official and public opinion alike.

The secondary technical school   What on earth happened to the secondary technical schools? As one of the props in a shaky tripartite system their distribution was at best sporadic, but at the beginning of the period there were well over 300 of them. By 1968 their numbers had dropped to less than 100, since when they have quietly faded out of the picture. Strange, this, because the technical school's close connections with industrial and commercial enterprises made it vocationally attractive and its course offerings in many ways more realistic than those of either the grammar or the modern school. Today, when once again the cry is raised for closer links between the work of the schools and the requirements of the labour market, its demise may well be rued.

As a serious contender for a place in the tripartite system, unfortunately the technical school was never given much of a chance. In 1947 *The New Secondary Education* had hailed it as the equal of the grammar school, catering 'for a minority of able children who are likely to make their best response when the curriculum is strongly coloured by [industrial and commercial] interests, both from the point of view of career and because subject matter of this kind appeals to them'. The snag was that most technical schools admitted entrants at the age of twelve or thirteen, by which time likely lads and lasses who had been offered special places in grammar schools had already accepted them. Except as a second chance for those who had narrowly failed the 11-plus test, the technical school's later age for transfer was a serious handicap. A further disadvantage was that more often than not it shared its accommodation, equipment and staff with a technical college intended for mature students. It suffered from a chronic shortage of teachers who had been specially trained to deal with adolescents.

Above all, the sheer indifference with which all but a few L.E.A.s regarded the secondary technical school and their readiness to allow it to relapse into desuetude must be ascribe to the British dislike of seemingly banausic educational services. This snobbish dislike is one of the less admirable legacies of Hellenism and a vice for which the nation has paid dearly. Whatever the reason, the technical school ceased to exist as a separate entity.

The grammar school   As late as 1938 less than half the pupils in
grammar schools were holders of free places. After World War II
the proportion of first-generation pupils, i.e. chidren whose
parents had never attended a secondary school, was much
higher. This change in the composition of its clientèle goes a
long way towards refuting charges that the grammar school is
essentially a middle-class institution. Frances Stevens' point is
wittily taken:

> 'Working' and 'middle' classes are by no means so clearly
> definable as writers on social and political subjects are apt to
> suggest. Income cannot be the determinant: even though
> working-class earnings tend to be exaggerated in the general
> opinion, they nevertheless often exceed those of 'clerical
> grades' .... Did W.H. Davies, we may wonder, belong to the
> middle class because he was a poet, or the working (or non-
> working) class because he was a tramp? Is a watch-maker
> working-class because he works with his hands and the man
> who runs a betting shop middle-class because he does not? Is
> the distinction, rather, between employers and employed?
> Then the shop assistant, the teacher, the clerk are all working-
> class.[14]

The question, however, is not simply whether the grammar
school's intake is more socially mixed than it used to be. A much
more pertinent question to ask is, 'How many are taken how
far?' If the phenomenal increase in the numbers reaching the
O-level stage is cause for congratulation, the fact remains that
socioeconomic factors still make it a good deal easier for children
from managerial, professional and clerical home backgrounds to
stay on beyond that stage than it is for children whose parents
follow unskilled or semi-skilled occupations. If the grammar
school has the edge over other types of secondary school it is
because it has always been end-on to the university. Those who
patronized it did so on the understanding that, *of course*, pupils
would stay on for two years in the sixth form; and that a school
life dedicated to scholarship would bring its rewards not only be
conferring upon them the hallmark of a liberal education but
also by opening the way to 'positions of considerable emolument',

as Dean Gaisford said of the Classics. To the extent that its main interests were reserved for those who stayed on beyond the O-level stage, then, it might be more accurate to say that the grammar school served an upper middle class. If the independent sector was reserved for protégés of a ruling class, the nineteenth-century grammar schools catered for the next-in-line cadres in the social hierarchy, modelling themselves on the image of the Public Schools. Thus, they had house systems and prefects, forms (not standards), masters (not teachers), scholars (not pupils.) Their broad-based curriculum provided the training for the Christian gentleman and the Man of Culture. Culture with a capital C, indeed, was thought to be the proper business of the grammar school — and so far as the statutory school system was concerned, its exclusive property. *Noli me tangere* was its motto and superscription.

Now that the grammar school is on the defensive, the argument that it should be preserved because it has served the nation so well in the past begins to look a trifle thin. Steam locomotives also served the nation well in the past but no one wants to see them preserved except as museum pieces.

> Traditionally, education has been concerned with the task of cultural transmission and the culture in question has been that of a minority group. It has been the duty of the schools to preserve this culture — the best that has been thought and said — and to hand it on reverently to an élite class. During the twentieth century this élite has rapidly increased in size, and the grammar school in particular has extended its influence into new areas of society. For years, too, it has been becoming apparent that in a highly concentrated and technological society new conceptions of the functions of education must replace the old. The schools can no longer confine themselves to the business of handing on an unchanged, or even a slowly changing body of information and attitudes. [15]

In expanding its intake and in broadening its range of studies to include elements of scientific and technological culture as well as those of Arnoldian literary intellectualism, the grammar school has done its level best to reconcile the conflicting claims of general and special education. Fears that early specialization might have insidious side-effects came to a head in 1959 after C.P. Snow's Rede Lecture on 'The Two Cultures and the Scientific Revolution' which suggested that 'at the top of the Establishment' the communication gap between Arts men and scientists was virtually unbridgeable. In the same year the Crowther Report, *15 to 18*, deplored the pressures on pupils to drop important subjects at the ages of fourteen or fifteen when the routes leading to an Arts or Science sixth form diverged, but decided that specialization was here to stay: 'Today an all-round education is possible only at a relatively low level.' While acknowledging that the concentration on a narrow range of advanced studies which characterized the work of the English sixth form was not to be found anywhere else in Western Europe, it thought that its worst excesses could be mitigated by the judicious use of 'minority' time, i.e. time not earmarked for examination purposes. 'We attach great value to the English practice of specialisation. Equally, we attach great importance to those complementary elements in the Sixth Form curriculum which are designed to develop the literacy and science specialists and the numeracy of arts specialists'[16].

But if it was satisfied with the superlative qualities of grammar-school education at its brilliant best, the Crowther Report's analysis of the sociological evidence in the Survey of National Service Recruits had more dismal implications. Only twelve per cent of the boys and girls came from homes in which both parents had received a longer education than the legal minimum. Among families of manual workers it was still the exception for pupils to stay at school beyond the minimum leaving age. The inference was clear and bluntly stated: 'This report is about the education of boys and girls aged from 15 to 18. Most of them are not being educated …. If we are to build a higher standard of living — and, what is more important, if we are to have higher standards in life — we shall need a firmer educational base than we have today'[17].

Nasty thought: could this mean that the education of the few was being subsidized at the expense of the many? Had England been putting too many of its eggs in one basket, lavishing resources on the one type of secondary schooling which enjoyed a monopoly of social esteem? And was the ethos of the traditional grammar school's culture somehow out of sympathy with the subculture of many first-generation pupils?

As regards this last point, the guilt complexes and personal dilemmas so harrowingly described in some of the individual case studies in *Education and the Working Class* need not be taken too seriously: on the whole, first-generation grammar-school pupils settled in easily enough and survived the process of re-socialization without experiencing any pangs of conscience as a result of 'changing their class'. In a study of one grammar school reported in 1969, 63.2 per cent of first-generation boys had fathers in manual occupations[18]. In any case, the emergence of a newly affluent working class in the late 1950s meant that many more parents than ever before were in a position to encourage their children to remain at school as long as possible. So insatiable was the demand for paper qualifications that G.E.C. results were widely regarded as the sole criterion for a pupil's, a teacher's or a school's success.

Much more disturbing was Lacey's participant observation study in *Hightown Grammar* which showed that the internal organization of a selective secondary school had the effect of polarizing the attitudes of pupils with roughly the same measured ability at 11-plus and from roughly the same social backgrounds. Previously it had been thought that pro-school and anti-school subcultures were accounted for by influences in the external environment. According to the Lacey model, streaming could produce them *ex nihilo* in the space of two years.

Yet however many may have been choked off, the trend towards a longer school life continued. Slowly, that is. By 1968-9 the number of school-leavers in the United Kingdom with at least five O-levels (O-grades in Scotland) have reached 172,700, although the number with at least two A-levels (three H-grades in Scotland) was only 89,500[19]. The abrupt cut-off after age 15, the minimum leaving age, was reflected in the low percentages of the age groups in full-time attendance — 34 per cent of 16-year-olds, 19.1 per cent of 17-year-olds and a mere 6.7 per cent of 18-year-olds. Ten years after Crowther it could still be said that the vast majority of the 15-18 population was not being educated. By 1973 the situation was somewhat improved, with 28.8 per cent of 17-year-olds receiving full-time education. Of these, 7.1 per cent were in grammar schools, 1.7 per cent in direct-grant schools, 4.2 per cent in independent schools, 7.8 per cent in comprehensive schools, 8.0 per cent in technical colleges and 0.7 per cent in modern schools[20].

Until the early 1960s most 16-18 students were members of sixth forms in maintained grammar, direct-grant and indepenent schools. Throughout the post-war era the sixth form had grown bigger and bigger — so top-heavy in some of the super grammar schools as to account for half their enrolments — until in the end it showed signs of developing as an institution in its own right. In the process of hiving off from the rest of the school, its whole character underwent a sea-change. As the keystone in the grammar school's structure it had always prided itself on being highly academic. Admission to it was reserved for those whose performance in the G.C.E. O-level examination indicated that they were capable of pursuing in-depth studies for A-levels or for university scholarships. In direct-grant grammar schools this is still the case. Not so in the new-style sixth forms which no longer answer to the Crowther description, i.e. in having close links with the universities, subject-mindedness, intellectual discipleship between teacher and taught, and social responsibility — though it is fair to say that the traditional insistence on the need for independent study remains. Today it might be said that a sixth former is simply someone who is at least in his sixth year of secondary schooling, not necessarily in a grammar school. He may be resitting for O-level G.C.E. or even C.S.E., or staying on for the C.E.E., and possibly has no intention of proceeding to the university. More socially mature and responsible than his predecessors, he wants to be treated in a more adult way than is normally allowable under school regulations, wants more time to shop around for a satisfying career, more freedom. At a time when the authorities are crying out for more applied scientists he is inconsiderate enough as to be more inclined to be interested in arts and social studies. The kind of privileges and responsibilities afforded by the old prefectorial system have less appeal than they once had: when it comes to displaying social responsibility his allegiance is to the world outside the school. While there is no evidence that this outlook has been influenced by a disaffected and restive youth culture, there is a good deal of evidence to suggest that his readiness to remain in *statu pupillari* is due to developments in the juvenile labour market which have made secondary schooling come to seem no better than a pointless waiting game for many teenagers who are not academically inclined.

A Schools Council survey (1970) in which more than 4,000 sixth formers and their teachers in 154 schools were interviewed, analysed the reasons given for thinking that staying on for a sixth form course was advantageous[21]. Asked to rate the importance of different aspects of the course in rank order, the teachers voted for (1) independent study, (2) information about higher education, (3) clear written expression, (4) personality and character and (5) questioning attitude. For their part, sixth formers' rankings were more directly concerned with career prospects: (1) careers information, (2) information about higher education, (3) independent study, (4) A-level success, and (5) wide subject choice.

Originally, the sixth form was an integral part of the grammar school. As such it has always been defended on the grounds that its achievements are so splendid that any attempt to detach it from the main body would be an act of senseless decapitation. Without its crowning glory the grammar school would be left like a headless chicken or a blind Samson. This kind of argument, it should be added, cuts no ice at all in Scotland where the sixth form never existed anyway.

The democratization of the sixth form, however, has created its own economic problems and these in turn have reinforced the hiving-off process. Unit costs at this stage had always been high — £332 per capita in 1970. As the numbers multiplied many L.E.A.s organized *sixth form centres* serving a consortium of short-course (11-16) secondary schools in the area. Others planned Sixth Form Colleges in which the physical separation from the grammar school was complete both as regards premises and the specialist staff employed in them. Some allowed open access, others imposed nominal entrance requirements.

Beyond saying that the provision of upper secondary education has become more diversified and that the grammar school's share of it has diminished, the present institutional framework can only be described as fluid, makeshift and complex. Ronald King summarizes the emergent situation:

> This expansion of education for the 16-19 age group has been accompanied by an increase in the number of forms of educational organisation catering for them. In the early 1960s most of these students were members of sixth forms in maintained grammar, direct grant and independent schools. Ten years later less than half of the seventeen year olds attended such schools. The rest went to technical colleges or colleges of further education, and comprehensive schools of several different kinds. These include the all-through schools with an integral sixth form, sixth forms in upper schools with recruitment at twelve, thirteen or even fourteen, sixth form colleges catering for post-16 students only, and sixth form centres where the sixth form recruits not only from its own fifth year but also from those of other schools.[22]

The situation is rendered the more complicated by the blurring of lines of demarcation between 'secondary', 'further' and 'higher' education, each of which has a sphere of influence that eludes exact definition. It seems to be only a matter of time before these new-style institutions are designated as Open Colleges. Significantly, for the sake of economy, some of them are housed in disused grammar schools. To that extent, the top floor of the selective secondary school has been removed — another way of saying that it has 'gone comprehensive'.

10/65: the way ahead

Between 1960 and 1974 the number of grammar schools was reduced from 1,284 to 675 (including a hard core of 176 direct-grant schools). During the same period the number of secondary modern schools declined from 3,887 to 1,509, while the number of technical schools fell from 228 to thirty-five. In 1950 there were ten comprehensive schools, 130 in 1960 and 2,273 in 1974.

The bare figures give as good an indication as any of the remarkable transformation which took place during the 1960s and early 1970s. These were the boom years when for the first time educational expenditure exceeded that for any other services of welfare statism, including defence. Previously, any adoption of the comprehensive principle had been so slow and uncertain as to raise doubts about the possibility of its ever being formulated as a national policy. Not that it has all been plain sailing since 1965 — the political in-fighting between those who cry 'Forward' and those who cry 'Back', has continued unabated — but advances on a broad front have certainly been easier since the issue of the D.E.S. Circular 10/65. This requested all L.E.A.s to submit plans for comprehensive reorganization and listed six acceptable forms which these plans might take:

(1) 'all-through' comprehensives with an age range of 11-18
(2) a two-tier system of junior comprehensives with transfers for all pupils to senior comprehensives at 14 or 15
(3) a two-tier system of junior comprehensives with transfers for *some* pupils to senior comprehensives at 13 or 14
(4) a two-tier system of junior comprehensives with transfers for *some* pupils at 13 or 14 to one of two types of secondary school, only one of which provided courses beyond the leaving age
(5) short-course comprehensives with an age range of 11-16 with transfer for *some* pupils to Sixth Form Colleges
(6) a three-tier system with transfers for all from primary schools at 8 or 9 to middle schools with an age range of 8/9-12/13 followed by senior comprehensives.

It was pointed out that options 3 (the original Leicestershire Plan) and 4 were not fully comprehensive since they involved the segregation of children after 13 or 14 and that they could only be approved as temporary measures. The circular made it clear that the Department's preference was for the 'all-through' formula though it recognized that plans made on this basis would be

difficult to implement in the short term. It was tactfully silent
on the vexed question as to how comprehensives were to coexist
with selective grammar schools.

It would be wrong to imagine that 10/65 marked a sudden
change of policy or to see it as an attempt to pressurize L.E.A.s
who wanted to hang on to their grammar and modern schools,
though the document can be seen as a turning point, if not as a
breakthrough. In effect, all it did was to bestow official blessing
on a piecemeal process of reorganization which had been going
on for several years and which it hoped to see speeded up and
become more general. As the authors of *Half Way There* rightly
remarked,

> Enthusiastic governmental and departmental backing for
> comprehensives in the 1950s was not conspicuous, as the
> failure to reach even the modest target figures of the 1945
> development plans suggest .... Where any pioneering was
> done, it was due to progressive local authorities, both Labour
> and Conservative controlled. It was to local authorities, then,
> relayed by the Inspectorate, that the government and the
> Department of Education and Science (D.E.S.) turned when
> it came to drawing up circular 10/65. All six of the schemes
> suggested were either in operation or proposed through local
> authority initiatives. The 'central guidance' that 10/65
> claimed to give in effect amounted to passing round to all
> authorities what the D.E.S. found in its suggestion box in
> 1965.[23]

By 1970 most L.E.A.s — 129 out of 163 — had implemented
comprehensive schemes or produced acceptable scenarios. On
the face of things this appeared to be rapid progress: unfortunately it takes at least six years to complete the feed-through
process of reorganization — and seventy-four per cent of the
children in English L.E.A.s were still in grammar, technical or
modern schools. Moreover, 137 L.E.A.s still retained their
11-plus selection procedures. To radical ways of thinking the rate
of advance was far too slow.

In pressing for a clear, positive and national decision in favour
of an all-out, all-in, all-through comprehensive system and for

alternative plans.

legislation to make it compulsory, *Half Way There* drew up a formidable list of requirements. Among others, these included making secondary education available for all up to the age of eighteen, putting an end to academic and social selection, more money for building, more generous provision for schools in need of special support, more freedom of choice for parents within the framework of an all in system, more pastoral care and guidance, replacing G.C.E. and C.S.E. with a common course leading to a single examination at the age of sixteen, elected representatives of parents, staff and senior pupils on governing bodies, more community control and more public scrutiny of decisions taken by the D.E.S. and L.E.A.s.

A tall order, as Caroline Benn and Brian Simon were the first to concede:

> Quite obviously the lines upon which many feel genuine comprehensive schools should develop, and towards which many are already working, will take time to achieve. What we have set out are long-term goals, not measures of achievement. But at the same time we have shown that a remarkable number of comprehensive schools have already attained many of these goals. It makes the failure of so many authorities to experiment with a single comprehensive school seem all the more retrograde. It also underlines dramatically the severe inequalities that still exist in Britain — with students in some authorities guaranteed access to full educational opportunity while students in other authorities are still being labelled a 'success' or a 'failure' at the age of eleven or twelve and shunted into schools with limited courses and a narrow range of subjects. This half and half system cannot be allowed to continue indefinitely.[24]

In the fervour of righteousness sparked off by a 'white heat of technological revolution' which was soon to be left cooling its heels, this impatience with what seemed like delaying tactics on the part of many L.E.A.s was understandable but perhaps misguided. With so many intractable problems awaiting solution it was inevitable that a half-and-half system would continue for a very long time. Labour's 1970 Education Bill which sought powers for the Secretary of State 'to *require* local authorities to submit one or more plans for going comprehensive', was rejected in committee largely because of Labour backbenchers' abstentions, and in the June election of that year a Conservative government was returned to power. As Britain's economic crisis worsened and money became tighter, reforms which had been demanded as necessities in the 1960s came to be seen rather as desiderata after 1970 and postponed *sine die*. If Margaret Thatcher's Circular 10/70 (revoking 10/65) did little more than slow down the already slow process of reorganization, Labour's determination to speed it up by threatening legislation to enforce it was to prove no less abortive, culminating in 1976 in a *cause célèbre*, D.E.S. versus Tameside L.E.A., in which the Law Lords decided that the Secretary of State had exceeded his powers. There the matter rests, awaiting resolution in a new Education Act.

Seeing that five of the six schemes listed in 10/65 mentioned junior comprehensives, was it really practical politics to recommend the all-through comprehensive as the orthodox solution? Quite apart from the English horror of mammoth schools, might not a common short-course reorganization on the lines of the French Collège d'Enseignement Secondaire or the Italian Scuola Media have proved to be more workable and expeditious? With the leaving age due to be raised to sixteen in 1972-3 the opportunity existed, though to have taken it would have meant leaving the problems of the upper secondary school to be tackled later, something which the 'all-through' proponents were not prepared to contemplate.

The argument was, of course, that if the school was to have a sizeable sixth form it needed to have an enrolment of between 1,000 and 2,000 — not a very plausible argument in view of the observed tendency towards separate provision for the 16-19 age groups. Rather more cogent was the argument that optimal utilization of resources was only possible by concentrating staff and equipment on the same site. The possibility that any economies of scale effected in this way might be prejudicial to the human scale — prejudicial in the sense that the internal organization of an outsize school might become so intricate as to

make interpersonal and interdepartmental communication difficult and to leave many youngsters lost in its mazes — was not
seriously entertained at the time. Whether it was high-rise flats,
hypermarkets, airports or schools, the assumption was that
planning developments necessitated big thinking and big
spending. Something of the spirit of 'bigness and bedamned-
ness' which afflicted the American high school at its nadir in the
early 1950s infected the enthusiasm for bulldozing reform in
British education a decade later. In the U.S.A. second thoughts
were precipitated by the Sputnik scare; in Britain by the oil crisis
fifteen years later.

That second thoughts about the wisdom of the 'all-through'
solution would eventually be necessary becomes clear if the
objectives of the comprehensive school laid down by the working
party which advised the Secretary of State in 1965 are broken
down and analysed in detail. These objectives were:

(1) (a) To eliminate separatism in post-primary education by
(b) gathering pupils of the whole ability range in one
school so that (c) by their association pupils may benefit
each other and (d) that easy readjustments in grouping
and subjects studied may be made as pupils themselves
change and develop.

(2) (a) To collect pupils representing a cross-section of society
in one school, (b) so that good academic and social
standards, (c) and integrated school society and (d) a
gradual contribution to an integrated community beyond
school may be developed out of this amalgam of varying
abilities and social environments.

(3) (a) To concentrate teachers, accommodation and equipment so that pupils of all ability groups may be offered a
wide variety of educational opportunity and that (b)
scarce resources may be used economically. [25]

Laudable as each and all of these objectives are in principle, it is
easy to see why sceptics are convinced that some of them are
unattainable in practice. The inherent difficulties in these
general statements of aim call for closer consideration.

Eliminating separatism

If a common-core curriculum is to be established its foundations must be laid in the first two or three years of the course. Given the large intake of an 'all-through' comprehensive with an eight- or ten-form entry, the practice of allocating pupils to different streams, sets or bands on the basis of their gradings in the primary school seems likely to continue indefinitely.

> Whether division is in descending order of ability or in bands, each form has to have a description or a name, bringing up the problem of pupils themselves appreciating their grading. In answer to a question about trying to conceal from pupils the implication of ability-distinction, one correspondent wrote, 'What would be the point? They all know within twenty-four hours'.[26]

A 1968 N.F.E.R. survey revealed that only 4.5 per cent of the 331 schools in the sample had completely mixed-ability groups in the first year, against 83.4 per cent which were divided into streams, bands or parallel forms.[27] Anomalies of this sort invite the mocking criticism that comprehensives merely disguise the old selection procedures without in any way eliminating them. The argument, it is said, is circular and self-defeating: 'A differentiated education, given in separate schools, is undesirable because only a grammar school education is worth having. Therefore all kinds of children must go to the same school. But their endowments and needs differ: therefore they must have within the school — a differentiated education. This is where we came in[28].

Latterly, unstreaming has been shown to be more practicable than its opponents have maintained, yet professional opinion remains unconvinced. Many graduates freely admit that they are at a loss when it comes to handling mixed-ability groups. As specialist subject teachers, the training they have received has not given them the necessary competence or the confidence — nor do methods lecturers in the colleges and university departments of education have the expertise needed for courses of initial and in-service training. Bruner's hypothesis that any subject can be taught in some intellectually honest form to any child at any stage of development is too far-fetched to have any credibility in the conditions of learning and teaching in a mixed ability classroom. Mathematics is by no means the only subject which is often said to demand ability grouping. In the teaching of foreign languages unstreaming has been found to be ideal for the first year, beneficial for most of the second year, but quite untenable in the third year[29]. Coping with mixed-ability groups may be easier for non-graduates in some subjects but normally at levels well below the academic requirements for O-level work. Harmonizing the status differences and different teaching styles of grammar-type and modern-type staff poses yet another problem to which insufficient attention has been given.

In the aftermath of tripartitism, getting rid of the practice of streaming has proved to be all but impossible. The prejudice in favour of its retention is so strong and deep-rooted that no amount of research evidence is likely to dislodge it. In any case, so the argument goes, the evidence is open to widely different interpretations and can be discounted since it settles nothing. This is the blind-spot in our insular mentality. In 1962 a UNESCO report noted that the range of scholastic attainment in English schoolchildren was significantly wider than in any of the eleven other countries in the survey, and suggested that this was due to the fact that English educationists *expected* wide differences. Is there anything in the all-too familiar charge that streaming is a self-fulfilling prophecy? On prima facie grounds, certainly, the charge is difficult to refute: tell one child that he is a 'high-flyer' and another that he is a 'thicky' and the chances are that both will not only believe it but act accordingly. If programmed learning techniques proved anything at all it was that bright and dull pupils could both achieve the learning objectives set for them, though at very different rates. To date, alas, the positive reinforcement essential for slow learners has too often been lacking. There are no indications that 'by their association pupils may benefit each other': how could there be so long as the practice of keeping them apart for academic purposes remained the rule! Nor are there any indications that bringing them under the same roof has encouraged more below-average pupils to stay on longer than they did when they were housed in modern or junior secondary schools. In Scotland regular absenteeism among 14-15-year-olds is currently as high as forty per cent in some city comprehensives, proof that disaffection with formal schooling sets in long before the age of leaving. Since 1970 deschoolers have not been the only ones to question the efficacy and, indeed, the legality of compulsory attendance to sixteen, let alone eighteen.

But if the 'group at the bottom', like the poor, are always with us, there is no doubt that many more children have achieved a measure of success in leaving certificate examinations than would have been possible if they had remained in separate schools. It is a pity that O- and A-level performance should commonly be taken as *the* criterion of the success of a comprehensive school, particularly as it is left to compete on unequal terms with selective secondary schools, but even in this respect its track record is a good deal better than its detractors care to admit. Ultimately, the dialectic of events must result in a common leaving certificate: eliminating separatism cannot stop short at merging different types of school. At present, however, the Schools Council's plan for a common examination has been referred for future consideration by the D.E.S. — not the only hot potato to be placed in cold storage. The reluctance to recognize the Certificate of Extended Education (C.E.E.) even after a pilot run lasting seven years suggests that academic/nonacademic separatism is unconscionably hard of dying. It remains to be seen whether the sociologists' new interest in the curriculum will bring about a different persuasion. As it is,

> the contemporary British education system is characterized by academic curricula based on a selection of knowledge which has high social status. It follows, therefore, that for the teachers (and probably the children) high status is associated with areas of the curriculum that are (a) formally assessed, (b) taught to the 'ablest' children and (c) taught in homogeneous groups.[30]

Concerning the second objective, 'to collect pupils representing a cross-section of society in one school', the objections continue to come thick and fast. The usual objection that comprehensives stand for uniformity, not diversity, and to that extent represent a denial of parents' rights to send their children to schools of their own choice may be dismissed as hypercritical: in the past the vast majority of parents were in no position to exercise their rights to choose a full-length secondary education for their children. On the other hand, the objection that the reasons for wanting a social mix are doctrinaire, and that zoning of the catchment areas so as to include children from well-to-do suburban as well as those from slum-clearance districts is an arbitrary and messy way of bringing it about, is not so easily dismissed. The riots caused by bussing in Boston and other American cities should be a stern reminder that this is a potentially explosive issue. Social mixing may be all very fine in theory: in practice it stirs up more trouble than it is worth. What *is* a representative cross-section of society after all? Not one to be found in a comprehensive school catering for girls only, for boys only, or in one reserved for members of a particular religious denomination. Besides, if the intention is to create a community school, no power on earth can prevent the inequalities of West End and East End being reproduced in the long run.

All credit, then, to L.E.A.s which have made the best of a bad job with zoning schemes which, in the nature of things, are bound to be imperfect. All credit, too, to those headteachers who, against all the odds, have persevered with unstreaming. Where purpose-built comprehensives exist there are encouraging signs that the all-in ideal carries within itself the promise of its eventual fulfilment. John Sharp's *'Open School'*[31], Eric Midwinter's community school, and Tim McMullen's Countesthorpe College are but three of the many pointers to the shape of things to come. Elsewhere, the appalling difficulties encountered in shotgun marriages of grammar and modern schools and in trying to operate split-site comprehensives have not been overcome and have led to accusations of gerrymandering which are not entirely unjustified.

But what chiefly gives rise to misgivings is the thought that the objective of achieving 'good academic standards' may be hopelessly compromised by the insistence on achieving 'good social standards'. Rightly or wrongly, the feeling persists that only the first is 'educational'; and the fear is that the effect of any common course will be to enable the less able to do rather better than they did before and the gifted ones considerably worse. In other words, unstreaming will reduce the spread of scholastic attainment but only by a regression towards the mean. It is at this point more than any other that the value judgements of élitists and egalitarians are at loggerheads.

Kelly's comment is pertinent here:

> There are two things that can be said about this. The first of these is that we should perhaps be asking ourselves whether, even if this picture which the evidence presents is an accurate one we ought to be willing to purchase the academic education of a few 'gifted' children at the cost of the social education of all pupils. This is a question that should give us pause and many schools which have abandoned streaming have done so as a result of giving a positive answer to it. They have accepted that the social education of their pupils is every bit as important as the academic. Whatever position one takes on that issue, however, the second point is a more positive one. It is by no means certain that in the evaluation that has been undertaken of unstreamed schools we have been testing schools in which the methods of teaching mixed ability classes have been fully worked out. This kind of teaching is a highly complex matter and we should not be surprised if it takes teachers a long time to perfect it. The evidence that the very bright have not been adequately catered for in unstreamed classes should not lead us to believe that their needs cannot be attended to, not at least until considerably more attention has ben given to the development of appropriate methods for teaching such classes.[32]

Moonshine, retort the academics. If social education is held to be so important how to explain the fact, which appears to be a fact, that hooliganism and vandalism are increasingly rampant inside and outside the classroom? The outcry in 1976 over the phasing out of the direct-grant schools, which were given the option of going comprehensive or becoming self-supporting — as most of them elected to do — suggests that separatism will find its future expression in an enlarged independent sector at odds with the maintained system. Although it is true that only a handful of L.E.A.s are disposed to make a last-ditch stand against it, philosophically speaking, this England is little more than half-way there towards a wholehearted adoption of the comprehensive principle.

The education debate

Following Mr Mulley's ignominious rebuff in the courts the government's proposals for mandatory legislation were quietly shelved and D.E.S. policy became more conciliatory. In the chastened, slightly contrite mood of 1976 the new Secretary of State, Mrs Shirley Williams, was at pains to let it be known that she had neither the power nor the desire to resort to compulsion; and in his Oxford speech of that year the Prime Minister called for a national debate on education. The impression given was that it was time to call in the auditors, even to hold a post-mortem on grandiose plans which nearly everyone agreed had produced disappointing returns. To ask what had gone wrong was acknowledged to be an open question which could only be settled by a free interchange of views among all the parties concerned.

The government's and the Department's quandary was reflected in the decision to take soundings of professional and public opinion in a series of educational conferences. As an exercise in participatory democracy, this sounding-out process, like the more secretive one which preceded the publication of the 1943 White Paper, can be seen as a preliminary clearing of the ground for a new Education Act. What the outcome will be is at present a matter for speculation. So far as the future of secondary education is concerned, all that can be said is that the same tired old arguments for and against comprehensive reorganization are still being trundled out and that the polarization of left-wing and right-wing partisans is, if anything, more pronounced than it was when the issue first began to be contentious. Those who favour the retention of the selective principle are sure that standards of scholarship are steadily deteriorating, that indiscipline and anti-social behaviour are rife, and that moral values have been eroded — and that in some way or other this is all due to comprehensivation (dreadful word). For their part, advocates of non-selective schools are equally sure that the accusation of falling standards is part of a dirty-tricks campaign waged by the kind of people who invariably resist any broadening of educational opportunity. Each charges the other with being guilty of the politics of envy.

At the risk of wearisome repetition, it has to be stressed that the debate about the effectiveness of comprehensives is befuddled by cross-talk in which standards are referred to in two antipathetic senses. For élitists, 'standards of excellence' are referred to the high peaks of intellectual and academic prowess scaled by a small minority of gifted children. These, it is claimed, are the ones who are destined to be the nation's leaders and pacemakers in adult life, the ones who need and deserve to be singled out for advanced studies at an early age, and the ones who are being held back by being placed in mixed-ability classes. For egalitarians, on the other hand, the 'standards' that matter most refer to the level of achievement reached by the broad mass of children. In their view, the summits of 'excellence' so beloved by the élitist are only made possible for the few by keeping the great majority permanently pegged down at a level well below their potential attainment. They point out the appalling human wastage involved in all selective school systems: for example, out of every hundred pupils entering the German Gymnasium at the age of eleven, less than twenty succeed in finishing the course.

Although England is still in two minds about its comprehensive reorganization, and although Scotland has gone further and faster in that direction without encountering anything like the same opposition, there is no denying that criticism of the new order has recently become more vociferous in both countries. 'Measured against the dream, the reality is a failure', says an editorial in the *Journal of the Scottish Schoolmasters' Association*, a judgement endorsed by a report issued by the Inspectorate of the Scottish Education Department in 1976, and one which is almost certainly shared by specialist subject teachers who are ill-prepared to face the problems of a common-course curriculum. As to that, however, it is fair comment to say that professional opinion always and everywhere tends to be conservative. Thus, in France, the main opposition to reforms in the highly selective Lycée has come from the *agrégés*, teachers with the highest status and highest academic qualifications. In Sweden, likewise, the common objection that going comprehensive would inevitably lead to an all-round lowering of standards came from the teachers themselves.

It seems that a good deal of the current disillusion with comprehensive schools arises from the fact that we have expected far too much of them. Ushered in with high hopes that they would create equal opportunity for all, we forget that the main reasons for their adoption were ideological rather than educational. The lesson which might have been learned earlier is that the tail cannot wag the dog: the wrongs of an imperfect society are not to be righted simply by reorganizing its schools.

That the worldwide trend is towards a one-track system of secondary schools with open access to all comers is obvious enough. No less obvious are the reasons for that trend. Put simply, it is no longer possible to conduct the affairs of an advanced industrial society with the aid of a managerial class drawn from the traditional learned professions. The question is whether going comprehensive has helped or hindered Britain in securing the broader recruitment base which is needed if the country is to hold its own in the international field. In trying to answer that question it seems wiser to take note of the available research findings than to listen to the pronouncements of novelists and Black Paper pamphleteers, provocative as these usually are.

The trouble is that such research as has been carried out so far is in no way conclusive. As happened in the countless investigations into the effectiveness of programmed learning as against conventional methods of classroom teaching, experimental designs for comparing selective and non-selective schools almost invariably end by throwing in the towel and reporting 'No Significant Differences'. Guy Neave's *How They Fared* adduced some evidence purporting to show that reorganization had helped to improve the chances of working-class children gaining access to higher education, but this has subsequently been queried or rejected by other investigators. The complexities of the question are further compounded by invalid comparisons between the examination successes in selective and non-selective schools. No useful purpose is served by claiming that grammar schools are superior to comprehensives because seventy-eight per cent of the pupils in the former obtain three or more O-level passes whereas only twenty-two per cent do so in the latter. At the same time Julie Evetts scores a palpable hit when she points out that 'even if the argument that most of the present comprehensives were creamed of their best pupils is accepted and their results compared only with the results of secondary modern schools, the comprehensives do not appear to be producing better results'[33]. Or does she?

As Professor John Eggleston confesses, contradictions and dubieties in the evidence make it extraordinarily difficult to evaluate the performance of comprehensive schools to date. After reviewing the literature, he is driven to the gloomy conclusion that 'Comprehensive school reorganization has made little significant difference either in changing the pattern of attainment or in solving our social difficulties. We are almost certainly getting much the same kind of education output that we should have been likely to get in any case'[34].

Is the entire comprehensive issue an irrelevance, then? Would we have been better off if we had stuck to the old tripartite arrangements — and has wholesale reorganization been a colossal waste of time and money? Have the disturbances caused by large-scale innovation in what might otherwise have been a steady state in the schools system really been accompanied by a rapid decline in academic as well as social standards? Was the raising of the school-leaving age a mistake? As a delivery system for the initial education of the 16-18 age groups might not a computer-based multi-media Open Secondary School have been considerably less expensive and vastly more efficient? Sir Walter Perry, for one, is inclined to think so:

It may well be that the ultimate answer ... for all those who are ill-prepared for the Open University, will lie in the creation of an Open School or Open College which will offer courses only at the pre-university level. The qualifications of such an institution need not then be a requirement for the Open University any more than are A-levels. Yet they would be an indication to the prospective student that he or she was ready and able to embark on a higher programme, through the distance-teaching method. A very strong case could be made out for having started such an Open School before ever there was an Open University, but the idea was not politically viable at the time. It would have filled an even bigger social need, and that need is still clamant.[35]

Before jumping to hasty conclusions it may help if some account is taken of comparative studies, in particular the International Education Achievement projects, whose mastermind is Torsten Husén. Drawing on the I.E.A. data for mathematics and science in the various countries, Husén compared the achievements of selective and non-selective schools. Not surprisingly, he found that their criteria of evaluation differed, one attaching prime importance to the top ratings of the few, the other to the general level of performance of the majority of pupils. Using the most sophisticated techniques of statistical analysis, he was left in no doubt that 'When comparable proportions of the age groups are compared the élite pupils in comprehensive systems tend to perform as well as those in selective systems'[36] Sir Walter Perry makes much the same point:

> I believe that Ashby's 'thin clear stream of excellence' refers to a particular kind of excellence which is best described as the excellence of scholarship; and that there are many other kinds of excellence.... Thus we cannot segregate the thin clear stream of excellence in scholarship from the wide and muddy river of ability; one must go on providing opportunities for scholars to emerge — and emerge they will — and then, whatever their age or their background, one must nurture them.[37]

It is one thing to extol the virtues of centres of excellence in which an intellectual *crème de la crème* is given preferential treatment, quite another to pretend that these virtues would be lost and that the result would be uniform mediocrity if the cream were to be spread widely and thinly. To say that Manchester Grammar School's examination record is vastly superior to anything that a run-of-the-mill comprehensive can boast is rather like saying that a Formula One Ferrari is faster on the racetrack than the ordinary runabout. For the same price you get more mileage from fifty Minis than from one Ferrari. Countries like the U.S.A., Sweden and Japan in which something like eighty per cent of the school population stay on to the age of eighteen may not match the concentration of talent in a selective system — it is often said, probably correctly, that the average twelfth-grader in an American high school is two years behind his opposite number in a traditional English sixth form — but there is little doubt that in the long run their broadening of recruitment in the upper secondary school *has* paid dividends.

> For almost a decade [says Husén] it did not occur to anybody in Sweden that one cannot compare a comprehensive with a selective educational system solely in terms of their respective end-products. In the first place one has to evaluate the systems in terms of the price paid for their respective end-products. What is the attrition rate? In the second place, one must consider the 'productivity' of an educational system by asking, 'How many are brought how far?'[38]

On this reckoning, the holding power of a secondary school becomes one of the main criteria for judging it success or failure. So far as Britain, and especially Scotland, is concerned the question, 'How many are brought how far?', allows of no complacent answers. The sour response to ROSLA schemes suggests that a substantial proportion of teenagers have acquired a positive distaste for formal schooling and all it stands for. Given that the annual cost of keeping each pupil in full-time attendance is between £200 and £300, high rates of absenteeism are a cause for serious concern. No cost-benefit calculations are needed to prove that there must be better ways of spending public money than this. Unless alternative forms of provision are found, and found quickly, this malaise could eventually prove fatal to comprehensives which are 'all-through' only in name.

To quote Husén once more:

> We have shown that an élite comparable to that of an élite system can be cultivated within a retentive and comprehensive system. In the selective system, however, the high standard of the élite is often bought at the price of low accomplishments of the mass. Selection for the pre-university school takes place at an early age, and the majority of pupils are left to complete either an elementary school or a low-prestige program within the secondary school with virtually no chance to transfer to a university. In order to be able to assess the total yield we ought to measure the performances of students at the intermediate terminal point when compulsory schooling has been completed. Postlethwaite has used I.E.A. data to show that high retentivity is associated with higher 'yield'; that is, the majority of students in a retentive system tend to achieve better than the corresponding groups in a selective system. [39]

At a time when educational expenditure faces severe cuts the problem of low retentivity in comprehensive schools looks like being insoluble, especially in areas like Clydeside where social deprivation is worse than it is elsewhere in the United Kingdom. In the general loss of confidence which is at once the cause *and* effect of economic recession it may well be questioned whether upper secondary education can, or ought to, survive in its present form. The sudden fall in the birth rate, itself denoting a vote of No Confidence in the future, appears to have caught the planners by surprise — as recently as 1969 *Education Statistics for the United Kingdom* had predicted that it would continue to rise — and made nonsense of their calculations. One by one, the assumptions of expansionist policy-making have been falsified. A stagnant economy cannot absorb the surplus of school-leavers, students and teachers who have been encouraged to pursue their studies for the sake of qualifications which bear little or no relation to the occupational skills they need. As a consequence, the rate of return from escalating expenditure on the educational services has been negligible. In the aura of disgruntlement which surrounds the current debate there is a distinct possibility that the essential worthwhileness of going comprehensive will once again by placed at risk.

Yet in any period of transition there are bound to be growing pains. Even if it could be shown that there has been a significant falling-off in the attainments of pupils of both above-average and below-average ability, there remains the strong probability that any such decline is temporary. If we look at what happened in the American high school after 1900 when the tidal wave of non-college-preparatory students first engulfed it, it is easy to see why the frantic hullabaloo about a 'flight from scholarship' was raised at the time and for long afterwards. It has taken the American high school more than sixty years to stabilize itself and satisfy the criteria of comprehensiveness and retentivity. Now that it has done so it may be thought to enjoy the best of both educational worlds, qualitative as well as quantitative. True enough, the impossible *does* take a little longer.

References

1 T. Burgess, *A Guide to English Schools* (Penguin Books, 1964), p.78.
2 A.E.C., *Annual Report* (1946).
3 I.G.K. Fenwick, *The Comprehensive School 1944-1970* (Methuen, 1976), p.83.
4 R. Manzer, *Teachers and Politics* (Manchester University Press, 1970), p.19.
5 C.G.A. Bryant, review of Göran Therborn's *Science, Class and Society*, in *British Book News* (February 1977).
6 D. Lawton, *Social Change, Educational Theory and Curriculum Planning* (University of London Press, 1973), p.141.
7 ibid., pp.41-2.
8 Newsom Report, *Half Our Future* (H.M.S.O., 1963), ch.1, 3-8.
9 J.S. Maclure, *Educational Documents: England and Wales 1916-1963* (Chapman & Hall, 1965), p.279.

10 D. Holly, *Beyond Curriculum* (Hart-Davis, Macgibbon, 1973), p.38.
11 M.F.D. Young, 'Curricula and the social organization of knowledge', in R. Brown (ed.), *Knowledge, Education and Cultural Change* (Tavistock, 1973), p.355.
12 H.C. Dent, *The Educational System of England and Wales* (University of London Press, 1969), p.118.
13 W. Taylor, *The Secondary Modern School* (Faber, 1963), pp.160-3.
14 F. Stevens, *The New Inheritors* (Hutchinson, 1970), p.86.
15 H. Davies, *Culture and the Grammar School* (Routledge, 1965), p.150.
16 Crowther Report, *15 to 18* (H.M.S.O., 1959), p.274.
17 Ibid., ch.1, 3.
18 R.A. King, *Values and Involvement in a Grammar School* (Routledge, 1969).
19 *Education Statistics for the United Kingdom 1969* (H.M.S.O.).
20 *Statistics of Education* (D.E.S., 1961-73).
21 R. Morton-Williams *et al.*, *Sixth Form Pupils and Teachers* (Schools Council, 1970), p.122.
22 R. King, *School and College* (Routledge, 1976), p.12.
23 C. Benn and B. Simon, *Half Way There*, 2nd ed. (Penguin, 1972), p.56.
24 ibid., p.50.
25 T.G. Monks, *Comprehensive Education in England and Wales* (N.F.E.R., 1968), p.xi.
26 *Teaching in Comprehensive Schools* (Cambridge University Press, 1967), p.69.
27 ibid., p.103.
28 Stevens, op. cit., p.118.
29 A.V. Kelly, *Case Studies in Mixed Ability Teaching* (Harper & Row, 1975), p.198.
30 Young, loc. cit.
31 J. Sharp, *Open School* (Dent, 1973).
32 Kelly, op. cit., pp.10-11.
33 J. Evetts, *The Sociology of Educational Ideas* (Routledge, 1973), p.89.

34 S.J. Eggleston, 'Research and the comprehensives', *The Times Educational Supplement*, 24 January 1975.
35 W. Perry, *The Open University* (Open University Press, 1976), p.189.
36 T. Husén, 'The standard of the élite — some findings from the I.E.A. International Survey in Mathematics and Science', *Särtryck Acta Sociologica*, vol. 16, no. 4 (Stockholm, 1974).
37 Perry, op. cit., p.282.
38 Husén, loc. cit.
39 Husén, loc. cit.

4 The continuous process
– tertiary education

Lofty-minded as it professed to be, the Victorian 'Idea' of a University has much to answer for. J.S. Mill's airy pronouncement that 'It is not a place of professional education', was mischievous if only because it was historically inaccurate: from its origins in Bologna and Paris the medieval *universitas* was nothing if not an institution of higher learning which catered for professional interests. Mischievous, then, is not too harsh a verdict on the transcendentalism of thinkers such as Mill, Mark Pattison, Cardinal Newman and that ilk, seeing that it was based on a concept of liberal education which was appropriate only for a gentleman of leisure and wholly out of keeping with the realities of nineteenth-century industrial society. Not only did it help to perpetuate the engaging Oxford myth that the man who has read Greats, without having done anything so vulgar as to have undertaken any training, can turn his mind to anything, but it reinforced both the official and the popular belief that only the privileged or the exceptionally able were capable of completing a degree course successfully.

As happened with the grammar school at the secondary stage, the prestige and dominance of the university has proved to be something of a hindrance to the development of a rational system of higher education in Britain. Even today, when status distinctions between the various up-and-coming institutions of higher education are becoming progressively blurred, the university is loth to reliquish its age-old claims to preeminence or to face up to a future in which even its claim to be treated as *primus inter pares* will be challenged. Recent developments in the tertiary stage of the national system, still awaiting completion, may be seen as the inevitable follow-up of the split-level developments at the secondary stage. Since grammar schools were end-on to the university, and secondary modern schools to the world of work and further education, it is easy to see how the so-called 'binary system' of higher education came into being; easier still to see why it had to compromise between élitist and egalitarian principles.

From laissez-faire to state intervention

The academic community's jealously guarded autonomy has always been strongly resistant to change. The record shows that universities never move unless they are pushed by outside forces. Although state intervention was slow to make itself felt, cautious to a fault in remaining concealed until the need for it could no longer be denied, the series of moves made by the government, first through the University Grants Committee and later by the Department of Education and Science, give the lie to suggestions that expansionist policies in the 1950s and 1960s were largely haphazard and unplanned. Tracing these moves, it becomes apparent that the major decisions had been taken *before* the much publicized Robbins Report made its appearance in 1963.

The first Treasury funds for civic universities, a mere £15,000, date from 1889. Between 1935 and 1945 grants remained fairly constant at the £2 million mark, during which period the number of university students never exceeded 50,000, a smaller percentage of the age group than for any other European country of comparable size. In 1946-7, grants totalled £6.9 million (for a student population of 77,000 students).

As early as 1948 the Committee of Vice Chancellors and Principals recognized the ways in which the winds of change were blowing and agreed in principle that governmental intervention was both necessary and desirable:

> The universities entirely accept the view that the Government has not only the right but the duty to satisfy itself that every field of study which in the national interest ought to be cultivated in Great Britain is in fact being cultivated in the university system, and that the resources which are placed at the disposal of the universities are being used with full regard both to efficiency and economy.

By 1955-6 the grant had risen to £28 million, (for 94,000 students), and by 1965-6 to £122 million, plus an extra £80 million for non-recurrent grants. This exponential rate of growth in direct grants to the universities may be explained as the government's response to the rapidly growing pressure of demand for places, but impressive as the figures are they raise some awkward questions. Even allowing for changes in the value of money it is evident that from the mid-1950s onwards unit costs increased out of all proportion to the number of students. Compared with France and the U.S.A., certainly, unit costs per full-time undergraduate were exorbitant, not to say extravagant, with the result that each and every new target set for increasing the number of students —'from the Barlow Report's projection of 90,000 by 1948-9 to the Robbins Report's 390,000 by 1973 — proved to be seriously underestimated. In so far as the tendency was to put all the nation's eggs in one basket, concentrating resources on the one and only form of higher education which was seen to be 'respectable' in the eyes of the politicians and academics alike, there must, therefore, be some sympathy for Tyrrell Burgess's indictment of Robbins, harsh as it is: 'The committee did not evolve a policy: what it did was to accept historical trends and institutionalise them. In all this it was not only conservative: it was reactionary.'[1]

After a slow build-up during the 1950s when the University

Colleges affiliated to the University of London were at last granted full university status — Nottingham (1948), Southampton (1952), Hull (1954), Exeter (1955), Leicester (1957) — the early 1960s witnessed a sudden and unprecedented boom in expansionist policies. Ever since 1954 the U.G.C. had been busy estimating the effects of the Bulge (i.e. the rise in post-war birth rates) and the Trend (i.e. the increasing tendency for secondary-school pupils, particularly those in grammar schools, to stay on until the age of 17-18 in the sixth form). In 1956 the U.G.C. had set a *minimum* target of 168,000 students to be reached by 1968. In the same year the designation of ten Colleges of Advanced Technology, earmarked for eventual recognition as universities, was a tacit admission that the existing foundations would not be able to satisfy the national need and that several new ones were required. From being no more than a buffer between the Treasury and the universities, a strengthened U.G.C. now became a planning agency in its own right and in 1959 set up its Sub-Committee on New Universities. This was followed almost immediately by the announcement that seven entirely new university foundations were to be approved.

The Plateglass Universities

While the rest of the country was waiting for Robbins, it is evident that powerful interests had been at work behind the scenes, nowhere more effectively than in Brighton where a group of highly influential backers ensured that Sussex was first off the mark in 1961. Proposals for York and Norwich had already been approved and by the end of 1961 those for Essex, Warwick, Kent and Lancaster had been added, whereupon the list was summarily closed.

'Intriguing' is the *mot juste* for the personalities and powers involved in the horse-trading that went on behind the scenes. Not surprisingly, for two or three years there was intense competition to secure charters, with local authorities vying with each other in their efforts to win the approval of the U.G.C. While attaching great importance to local enthusiasm and interest, the latter's choice among the various applicants pressing their case can hardly be said to have been even-handed, let alone disinterested. Fairly clearly, the odds were in favour of bidders who could offer spacious sites, preferably in cathedral towns or centres of historic interest well away from the murk and grime of densely populated industrial zones. *Procul o procul este, profani!* So Lancaster got the nod, not Preston or Blackpool (unthinkable!), and so, similarly, the one and only choice for Scotland went to Stirling, not Falkirk or Grangemouth.

Leaving aside for the moment the question of whether or not the giving of top priority to the 'Magnificent Seven' was justified in the circumstances, the arguments which seem to have weighed most heavily in the minds of the U.G.C. members at the time are worth considering. It was recognized, of course, that in the short term these new foundations would not be cost-effective, but it was felt that eventually they would be necessary if, as was confidently expected, the pressure of demand for university places continued to exceed the available supply. This, be it remembered, was the short-lived never-had-it-so-good era when ambitious schemes involving massive capital outlay and no expense spared could be launched without risk of public protest.

More cogent, perhaps, was the argument that the traditional organization of the existing universities, especially the Redbrick ones, with their separate, self-contained departments and single-subject honours courses needed updating, and that this could only be done by innovation-minded academics working in experimental institutions and in an entirely new context. 'Interdisciplinarity', 'contextual studies', 'Schools' — these were the catchwords of the day and the ones, it seems, which caught the ears of the U.G.C.

A more telling argument, never stated in public, was that a precedent and a prototype for the creation of new universities had been set at Keele, which began life as the University College of North Staffordshire in 1950 and which was allowed to award its own Bachelor's degree from the start, a privilege not previously accorded to other university colleges in the U.K. Unquestionably, Keele set the pattern for the future. In the first place, it was residential, designed to prove that 'small is beautiful', and it offered an undergraduate course in which the first year was devoted to the study of Western civilization and with three subsequent years spread over four subjects drawn from the natural and social sciences. As a preliminary injection of new blood into a somewhat humdrum tradition of university scholarship, Keele provided the model which took the fancy of the U.G.C. planners. In their judgement, the time had come for new universities to redress the balance of the old.

That the decision to go all-out for further injections of new blood was probably justified in the event is at least arguable. At the same time, these new Plateglass Universities cannot escape the charge that they aped the gentleman ideal and sought to preserve it in a grace-and-favour setting. All were born with silver spoons in their mouths. 'Balliol by the Sea', as a sardonic *Time* leader-writer dubbed Sussex, could hardly complain that the soubriquet was undeserved, however strenuously it might disclaim it as inappropriate, seeing that the Sussex ethos owed as much to Oxford's effortless superiority as its contextual courses did to P.P.E. To be fair, whatever other virtues the Plateglass Universities may have possessed, they were not lacking in elegance and panache. Each in its different way had *style*. Given that they were granted complete autonomy from the start and did not need to work their passage as the pre-war university colleges had been compelled to do, it was only natural that their new look should be accompanied by all the trappings of traditional ceremonial, not to mention a readiness to court the attention of Top People (Royalty whenever possible). To a man, their Vice Chancellors were distinguished Oxbridge scholars, go-getters all. Each planned his new foundation, if not in his own image, in cahoots with some modish architect, aided and abetted by the latest techniques of critical path analysis. If, in places, their best-laid schemes went agley, like those of most of the then-contemporary urban planners — as happened in the case of Essex where the hoped-for 'country club' atmosphere was virtually killed off from the start by a hideous tower-block complex of student residences — at least they lost no time in getting them off the ground. In asserting its novelty, each was determined not to appear in a second-best role. Each contributed an element of diversity which was badly needed in view of the rather lacklustre uniformity of the older civic universities. Now that the new models have been 'run in' it is hard to distinguish those of their features which are genuinely original and destined to endure and those which, to begin with, were over-preoccupied with image-building and ephemeral trend-setting. On the one hand, there is something to be said for Frank Kermode's view that they remain 'above all, a monument to the false optimum of the fifties, to the rediscovery of smartness and the charm of inequality'. On the other, a less jaundiced verdict is that of Max Beloff: 'Paradoxically, the Plateglass Universities which at the time of their creation seemed a luxury that we could afford now appear to be a necessity that we cannot'[2]. What is not in doubt is the fact that their genesis was lucky in its timing.

The Robbins Report

By 1965 the spending spree was over. In the previous year the U.G.C. had been transferred from the Treasury to the newly constituted Department of Education and Science which forthwith took a firmer grip on policy-making. In the meantime (1963) the long-awaited, not to say belated, Robbins Report had added massive support for the steadily growing demand for freer access to all forms of higher education. To this end, it recommended an immediate increase in the number of full-time students to 216,000, setting targets of 390,000 for 1973-4 and of 560,000 for 1980-1. It recommended that the volume of postgraduate studies and research should be considerably increased, that no time should be lost in designating the C.A.T.s as fully-fledged technological universities, and that a Council for National Academic Awards should be established with powers to award honours and pass degrees for students following courses in institutions which had yet to acquire university status. In general, most of the new universities needed to offset the acute shortage of places should, it believed, be sited near large centres of population and should include generous provision for scientific and technological students. In addition, besides giving a fillip to the lowly two-year (now three-year) training colleges by bestowing upon them the honorific title of Colleges of Education (what's in a name?) it wanted to see them brought into closer association with the universities as constituent members of Schools of Education, so as to enhance their standards and styles of teaching by interchanges of staff and joint boards of studies, and to safeguard the B.Ed. degree courses which many of them were to be allowed to initiate. While rejecting proposals for an all-graduate teaching profession as impracticable, it wished to see a big increase in the number of students taking four-year courses. Most of the colleges, it was felt, were too small and in the long run those with less than 750 students should be the exception rather than the rule. If the size of classes was to be reduced and a chronic shortage of teachers overcome, an annual intake of 40,000 students would be necessary. The colleges should have independent governing bodies and should be financed by earmarked grants made by a Grants Commission through the universities to the Schools of Education, — this with a view to strengthening the partnership between the two institutions.

As envisaged by the report, a single but larger Grants Commission would function on essentially the same lines as the existing U.G.C. but with powers and responsibilities covering the whole field of higher education, not simply the university sector:

> In the end we have come to the conclusion that for autono-
> mous institutions involved as they are not only in teaching but
> also in research and the advancement of knowledge, the most
> appropriate conjunction for the Grants Commission would be
> with the Research Councils, the Arts Council and other bodies
> that have the Status of advisory and distributing intermedi-
> aries. We recommend therefore the creation of a new Ministry
> with the responsibility for all such intermediaries with the title
> of Ministry of Arts and Science.[3]

While emphasizing that any estimates of the cost of this expansion were bound to be tentative, the Robbins Committee made its calculations on the basis of three assumptions, each of which, unfortunately, was falsified in the event. The first was that overall price levels would remain constant with any rise in incomes matched by corresponding increases in productivity (and we know what happened to that one!). The second was that the nation's productivity would show a 3 ½-per-cent increase per annum. The third was that,

> as an investment, there seems a strong presumption in favour of a substantially increased expenditure on higher education. Even if we cannot produce detailed computations of compara- tive yield, there is a strong probability that the country would have to go a good deal beyond what is contemplated in our recommendations before the return in terms of social net product could be said to suggest general over-investment in this sector.[4]

To its credit, the Robbins Committee took soundings among the leading economists of the day before plumping for the 'invest- ment in human capital' argument, though it cannot go for nothing that it was left to an American professor to expound (in Appendix Four, Part III) the pros and cons of the various techniques for investigating the nexus between educational expenditure and economic growth — a nexus which remains as problematical and baffling now as it was in 1963. To say that 'the increase in productivity arising from an increase in educa- tional expenditure does not lend itself to easy measurement', was putting it mildly, to say the least, besides putting the cart before the horse. In conditions of temporary affluence, appa- rently, the thought that any increase in expenditure could only be paid for by increased productivity was quietly suppressed. Instead, the Robbins philosophy expressed itself in such state- ments as 'Communities that have paid most attention to higher studies have in general been the most obviously progressive in respect of income and wealth', and

> To devote resources to the training of young people may be, *au fond*, as much entitled to be considered a process of investment as devoting resources to directly productive capital goods. Judged solely by the test of future productivity, a community that neglects education is as unprudent as a community that neglects material accumulation. The classical

economists, great supporters of education, had precisely this consideration in mind when they invented the phrase 'human capital'.[5]

On this kind of reckoning the estimated public expenditure on full-time higher education would increase from £206 million in 1962-3 to £742 million in 1980-1, and the total capital expenditure from £911 million in 1963-4 to £1,420 million. The Report admitted that these were 'big sums'. 'Can the country afford them?', it asked. 'Can it afford the still bigger sum representing not only the cost to the public purse but also all the other sacrifices involved by devoting resources to higher education on this scale rather than to other purposes?' In 1963 it was easy to silence the doubting Thomases with the counter question, 'Can they country afford anything less?' Ten years later both questions were fated to receive decidedly dusty answers.

By no means all of the Robbins recommendations were implemented, of course. The new Department of Education and Science preferred to keep the grant system more or less unchanged. The Schools of Education never materialized. But the powerful thrust given to the expansionist movement by the 1963 report on *Higher Education* and by the animated discussions which followed its publication cannot be overestimated. Of all its six weighty and data-packed volumes, none was more influential than Appendix One with its welter of statistical tables showing how social-class factors combined to create inequalities in educational opportunity and attainment. Here, once and for all, the myths of 'innate intelligence' and the 'limited pool of ability' were well and truly exposed and discredited.

Is it possible to tell what proportion of the population are so constituted at birth that, growing up under the most favourable circumstances, they could reach a level of attainment suitable for entry to higher education?

The answer is 'no': that is to say, one cannot specify an upper limit. There is, however, a great deal of evidence which suggests that the reserve of untapped ability in this country is still very considerable and that, on present trends, it is most unlikely to be fully mobilised within the next twenty years.[6]

Any idea that 'More means worse' was shrugged off with the curt statement 'Such evidence as exists does not support this view': on the contrary the average scores of university students in standardized verbal intelligence tests at Edinburgh and Liverpool, the only two universities where such tests had been regularly administered over a thirty-year period, showed a slight improvement. So effective, indeed, was this marshalling of sociological evidence in debunking the élitist mystique, hitherto so jealously guarded in academic circles, that for several years afterwards any attempt to defend it could be given its quietus simply by saying, 'But haven't you read Appendix One?'

That the chances of a doctor's or a lawyer's son being admitted to a degree course were twenty times greater than a ploughman's or a bricklayer's had always been taken for granted, if not exactly common knowledge. More so than any other single document, the Robbins Report announced what Sir Edward Boyle called 'the English sense of fairness' with its meticulous exposition of the hard facts of social-class deprivation. After 1963, then, the environmentalists and the egalitarians were in the ascendant.

Polytechnics and the binary system

1964 heralded the shape of things to come. The first move, previously noted, was the transfer of the U.G.C. from the Treasury to the Department of Education and Science, followed by the setting up of the Schools Council and the National Council for Academic Awards, a body with no formal connections with the university sector but empowered to grant external degrees and diplomas for students in non-university colleges.

The existence side by side of a university sector and a non-university sector marked a new departure in the evolution of higher education in England and Wales. The first had always enjoyed autonomy, if that is the word, at any rate to the extent of controlling its own internal affairs; the second was subject to the indirect control of the D.E.S., the Inspectorate and the L.E.A.s. Quite apart from the obvious status distinction, this dualism presupposed that same distinction between vocational-technical 'training' and liberal 'education' which had bedevilled theory and practice since Victorian times. A valid criticism of the Robbins proposals was that they took a partial view of what constituted higher education in so far as they saw it as dominated numerically and academically by the universities. No doubt this was partly due to the Committee's terms of reference which defined higher education in terms of full-time students taking degree courses (with the sole concession to include students in teacher training colleges working below this level). Be this as it may, the fact remains that more than 100,000 students on part-time courses at degree level in technical colleges of one kind or other and a further 100,000 students on courses below that level were excluded from serious consideration.

In his Woolwich speech (27 April 1965) the then Secretary of State, Anthony Crosland, outlined plans for a 'binary system' which were designed to bring the upper echelons of 'further education' more in line with 'higher education, so as to reduce the status differentials between them. The rationale of the speech was gently persuasive, if more than slightly reminiscent of talk of 'parity of esteem' between grammar and secondary modern schools in an early era.

> There is an ever-increasing need and demand for vocational, professional and industrially-based courses in higher education — at full-time degree level, *at full-time just below degree level*, at part-time advanced level, and so on. This demand cannot be fully met by the universities. It must be fully met if we are to progress as a nation in the modern technological world. In our view it therefore requires a separate sector, with a separate tradition and outlook within the higher education system.
>
> Secondly, … a system based on the ladder concept must inevitably depress and degrade both morale and standards in the non-university sector. If the universities have a 'class' monopoly of degree giving, and if every college which achieves high standards moves automatically into the University Club, then the residual public sector becomes a permanent poor relation perpetually deprived of its brightest

ornaments, and with a permanently and openly inferior
status ...

Thirdly, it is desirable in itself that a substantial part of the
higher education system should be under social control, and
directly responsive to social needs. It is further desirable that
local government, responsible for the schools and having
started and built up so many institutions of higher education,
should maintain a reasonable stake in higher education.

Fourthly, ... we shall not survive in this world if we in
Britain alone down-grade the non-university professional and
technical sector.

Fair words and well-intended, though prone to play fast and
loose with some of them. Still, it was no fault of the Minister's if
the terms used in this realm of discourse were by this time
slippery customers — 'degree level', 'sectors', 'social control',
'social needs', not to mention 'higher education' itself. Reading
between the lines, it is easy to detect the implied criticism of the
University Club as not being 'directly responsive to social needs'.
Bluntly, a binary system was the only way out of the dilemma
caused by spendthrift policies of expansion in which the lion's
share had been claimed by the universities. If further expansion
was going to be possible, a more economic deployment of
resources was necessary, even if it meant that the 'public sector'
figured in a second-best role. Above all, this sector was amen-
able to governmental control, capable of being 'managed' in
ways which had never been tolerated by universities.

As Martin Trow observed,

> While the question of authority for its own sake is undoubt-
> edly a political consideration, it is the concern with the
> preservation of genuinely 'vocational' institutions that lies
> behind much of the feeling for the binary solution. The
> question of relative costs is also involved. It is not only that
> the universities are by and large snobbish about vocational
> studies. It is also that their costs are so much higher than those
> of the 'non-autonomous' institutions that this alone places a
> real constraint on very rapid expansion within the university
> sector. Differences in operating costs between the universities

and the institutions of 'further education' (not including teacher training colleges), can be seen in figures provided in the National Plan. For the year 1964-65 current expenditure of all types for further education in England, Wales and Scotland (including student stipends) was £126 million. There were many different kinds of students in those roughly 150 institutions, but all together they were equivalent to 587,000 full-time students. The average expenditure per full-time equivalent in these non-autonomous institutions was a bit under £220. During the same year there were about 156,000 students enrolled in the 42 British universities and CAT whose operating expenses and student stipends came to £140 million, an average of about £900 per student.[7]

In 1966 the Secretary of State announced that thirty Polytechnics were to be designated by amalgamating some seventy colleges of technology, commerce and art to form 'comprehensive academic communities'. They were to offer courses at degree level, including higher degrees, as well as slightly below. They were to continue to accommodate part-time students and to concern themselves mainly with vocational and professional education, in other words to carry on in the technical college tradition. (In Scotland it was felt that the existence of the Central Institutions made new polytechnics unnecessary. In fact, some Scottish local authorities have submitted plans for polytechnics but to date none has been approved by the S.E.D.)

Despite early teething troubles, cheese-paring budgets and local disruptions caused by student militancy, the polytechnics have to a great extent succeeded in establishing themselves as 'separate but equal' alternatives to the universities.

In their range of course offerings and their standards of teaching and research they lose nothing by comparison with their big brothers, the erstwhile CAT, and they have every right to expect that sooner or later they, too, will be dignified with the title of universities. Yet their position in the hierarchy remains anomalous and their morale suffers from a certain inferiority complex. The sense of being a poor relation, aggravated by the 1968 and subsequent restrictions on local authority spending, irks them less than the accompanying sense of insecurity.

Not that the financial restrictions are the only ones under which they have laboured. Despite ministerial warnings not to ape the universities, the D.E.S. was not above imposing its will on the polytechnics, for example, in insisting on Liberal Studies being given their proper place. The fact that this exercise of benevolent dictatorship was enlightened in motive and salutary in its effects did not make it any less an infringement of academic freedom. From time to time the Ministry's Inspectorate took a hard line, as one college principal explains: 'They put the squeeze on in various subtle and not so subtle ways. Their normal role is to advise, persuade and suggest but, when occasion demands, they are adept at putting on a hammer lock and forcing submission.' Dr Brosan, Director of the North-East London Polytechnic, has characterized the conditions under which the colleges, including those offering advanced courses, are required to work as nothing less than the servile: 'The staff in the colleges, with a great deal of enthusiasm and efficiency, *operate a system that has been designed by some outside body.* That is, the great majority of teachers in the public sector of further and higher education are compelled, despite their abilities, to perform the function of technicians'[8].

Unnecessarily gloomy as this reading of the situation may be, there are reasons for thinking that the good, if vague, intentions of the 1966 White Paper have not been followed up with the necessary vigour or with anything like a consistent policy. As a result, the issues involved in the overlap between 'higher' and 'further' education remain as cloudy as they are contentious. In the meantime the polytechnics and colleges of higher education feed on the air, promise-crammed.

What the future holds for the 'public sector' remains to be seen. The irony of it is that the drastic financial cuts now being made are likely to be felt most severely in this sector, where they are least deserved, rather than in the universities, which are better-placed to bear them and which might well benefit from a regimen of austerity. When the economic blizzard blows, after all, the U.G.C. is a safer refuge than a penurious L.E.A.!

Asa Briggs' appraisal of this less than satisfactory state of affairs seems as just as any:

Public debate about the 'binary system' has been confused
for three reasons. First, it was never made clear whether the
system was considered to be an 'ideal' or an acceptance,
largely for economic reasons, of historical fact, involving the
'systematization' of what had hitherto been unsystematic
dualism or polycentrism in higher education. Second, the
bare economics of the systematization were never clearly set
out — relative costs, for example, in universities and polytechnics. Third, the implementation of policy was determined
largely by civil servants in discussions with local authorities,
and much that was happening was hidden from public view.
Although a higher education planning group was set up
within the Department of Education to consider the relation
between the different parts of the system, its work has been
confidential and its statistics have never been published.[9]

Waning enthusiasm

The D.E.S. had cause to be secretive. Had the cat been let out of
the bag the public disquiet concerning the extravagence and
misappropriation of the nation's dwindling resources might
have been aroused sooner and voiced more audibly than it was.

1968 was the Year of the Troubles. True, the sit-ins and
skirmishes at the London School of Economics, Hornsey College
and elsewhere were the merest storm in a teacup compared with
les évènements in Paris or the pitched battles on some American
campuses. For the most part, such protest as there was tended to
be good-humoured rather than violent. In Scotland scarcely a
whimper was heard from a student body notorious for its
unruliness at Rectorial ceremonies and its readiness to cock a
snook at authority. Still, as their numbers grew students found
less and less favour in the eyes of public opinion. Media exposure
did not help their cause: as depicted on the T.V. screen and
reported in the press their taking to the streets was counterpro-
ductive. Ebullience and a display of animal spirits might be
excusable on rag days but the spectacle of long-haired youths
carrying banners and shouting slogans simply did not square
with the man-in-the-street's notion of acceptable student

behaviour. Were not too many of them work-shy, more given to sex, drugs and political activism than to pursuing a life of scholarship, he was inclined to ask? Was it only a coincidence that most of the trouble-makers were the ones taking courses on sociology, political science and other new-fangled subjects? Grievances? But were they not a privileged, even a pampered minority — and did they not owe a debt of gratitude to society?

Many academics, likewise, took a poor view of the new generation of students, complaining that they lacked the necessary self-discipline, motivation and application for rigorous studies, to say nothing of respect for decorum. Different animals and no mistake! The generation gap which made communication between teenagers and their teachers and parents difficult was even more problematical at the level of higher education. To say that cultural changes in the post-war era had gradually eroded established values (regardless of whether these were referred to as religious belief, the Protestant ethic, conventional wisdom or a middle-class life-style) is a convenient way of glossing over our ignorance of the complex causes underlying these changes. All that can be said for certain is that, behaviourally, they manifested themselves in young adults generally as impatience with formality in any shape or form, as a determination to 'do their own thing' even when it meant throwing over the traces, and an aggressive assertion of their right to participate in the decision-making process. The teach-in, quite as much as the sit-in, was symptomatic of the new learning situation which they demanded. No longer content to sit at the feet of a master *in statu pupillari*, their inclination was to call upon the services of instructors as and when they felt the need for them. For a time it seemed as though the boot was now on the other foot, with students calling the tune and professors dancing to it, a state of affairs which was not altogether unprecedented seeing that it resembled the one existing originally at the University of Bologna.

In Britain, needless to say, the possibility of student power prevailing and overthrowing the established order was virtually non-existent. Even in Denmark where, for a time, students succeeded in browbeating the authorities into accepting their demands, including a veto on the content of courses and the abolition of graded examinations, the anti-establishment movement was short-lived and it was not long before the *status quo*, or something like it, was restored. University authorities might yield an inch or two of ground here and there, agreeing, for example, to set up staff-student committees for the airing of criticism and complaints or allowing elected student representatives to become members of boards of studies, but the truth is that when it came to system maintenance they were old hands at the game.

Dependent as they were on governmental grants, far more generous than those of any other country in the world, British university students were never really in a position to kick up much of a fuss. Any attempt to do so, therefore, was bound to seem like biting the hand that fed them. Although subject to a means test, grants were sufficient to ensure that all personal and tuition expenses were covered so that the great majority of students could live reasonably comfortably even during the long vacations. Poverty, at any rate, was no longer a bar to higher education. Whatever the National Union of Students might say to the contrary, public opinion in Britain was entitled to think that, by and large, those who remained in full-time education after leaving the secondary school were 'on a good thing'.

But how seriously, if at all, should we take suggestions that too many of them were work-shy? As to that, the verdict of an American observer whose opinion has to be respected may be relevant:

Most British students, I believe, do not have to work very hard to gain a reasonable degree, though I obviously will not endear myself to them for saying so. The examination system, especially at Oxbridge and the older universities, allows students extremely long periods in which self-discipline is the main impetus to work; but many students lack self-discipline. And the big examinations themselves are not as demanding as one might suppose except for the top degree classifications. A national survey in 1962 of students' work habits indicated that, according to the students themselves they worked an

average of 36.7 hours a week. The range was from 29.5 to
44.4 hours. The survey also indicated that very little work is
done in the long vacation periods given by British universities,
despite the state grants theoretically designed to cover such
work. Eighty-six per cent of the students said they studied less
than one hour a day during such periods. [10]

There is little doubt that a similar survey of the expanded
student population in the late 1970s would reveal a further
diminishing of student work-loads; and there is no doubt
whatever that the amount of intellectual effort involved in the
award of a first degree in Britain is a good deal less than that
required, say, in Eastern Europe.

Even more serious is the work-shyness which results from
educational inflation, the 'diploma disease' as Ronald Dore calls
it. Many graduates, realizing that their B.A. and B.Sc. degrees
qualify them for no particular profession — unless, of course,
they drift into teaching — prefer to stay on for further and
higher degrees in the hope of becoming research assistants and
eventually being appointed to the academic staff. Some do so
because they are cut out for a life of scholarship and research,
others are camp-followers who can think of nothing better to do.
Thanks to the fact that British universities have insisted, at all
costs as the saying goes, on keeping staff:student ratios lower
than is thought necessary in other countries, a fair proportion of
postgraduates continue to end up with academic appointments.
To some extent this increase in the size of staffs in explainable
as an effort to keep pace with the growth of the student
numbers, but not entirely. However undiplomatic it may be to
say so, many university departments are quite shockingly over-
staffed. Professorial empire-building is partly to blame for
this — the bigger the department, the greater the chances in the
scramble for research funds — but the real explanation is that
outside the shelter of academic circles many of the most highly
qualified young people nowadays are to all intents and purposes
unemployable.

As yet the spectre of graduate unemployment is not so
fearsome as it is certain to become once degrees become

progressively devalued. As it is, the possession of a first degree no longer carries with it the guarantee of salaried status and the free choice of some white-collar occupation. Sooner rather than later, disillusion is bound to set in as more and more graduates discover that they have to settle for humbler jobs than they have been led to expect — the kind of jobs, moreover, for which the higher education they have received must seem to have been largely irrelevant, if not a waste of time.

This competition for ever-higher qualifications is a process which feeds on itself, insidious because its effect is to treat learning and the mastery of skills merely as a means to an end, i.e. a passport to some coveted job.

The paradox of the situation is that the worse the education unemployment situation gets and the more useless educational certificates become, the *stronger* grows the pressure for an expansion of educational facilities. If you have set your sights — or if your parents have set your sights for you — on a 'modern sector' job, and if you find that your junior secondary certificate does not get you one, there is nothing to be done except to press on and try to get a senior secondary certificate, and if that doesn't work to press on to the university. The chances are that this will prove in fact to be a sensible decision. The mechanism of 'qualification escalation' ensures that once one is in the modern-sector-qualification range, the higher the educational qualification one gets the better the chances of getting *some* job.

The way the qualification-escalation ratchet works is roughly like this. A bus company may 'normally' require a junior secondary leaving certificate for £5-a-week bus conductors and a senior secondary leaving certificate for its £7-a-week clerks. But as the number of senior certificate leavers grows far larger than the number of clerkships that are available, some of them decide that £5 a week as a bus conductor is better than nothing at all. The bus company gives them preference. Soon all the available conductor slots are filled by senior certificate holders: a senior certificate has become a necessary qualification for the job.[11]

At the same time, it might be added, B.A.s preempt the clerkships — which from many points of view is absurd, but that's the way it is: O-levels, A-levels, first degree, Master's degree, Ph.D. Useless, apparently, for critics like Dore and Ivar Berg to diagnose it as the 'diploma disease' or to inveigh against the futilities of 'the great training robbery'. In advanced industrial societies employers and students alike are the willing dupes of the myth that formal schooling over a protracted period is an improving influence and, as such, an indispensable preliminary for entry into the world of work, *any* kind of work. Easy to forget that until quite recent times training for some professions — law, architecture, accountancy, as well as engineering — was undertaken almost entirely on *practical, work-based* lines without any formal degree qualification being thought necessary. Learning on the job had the advantage of being founded on first-hand experience, an advantage which is retained in the polytechnics' sandwich courses; the disadvantage was that it was *slow*. As the necessity for a thorough grounding in *theoretical* principles increased, however, membership of professional institutes could only be gained by passing a written examination and, before long, a three-four-year university course provided the most convenient short cut for school-leavers, exempting them from the hard graft of a long-drawn-out articled apprenticeship. As late as 1970, however, those wishing to become solicitors were advised that while a degree was an asset it could not be accepted as total exemption from apprenticeship as an articled clerk, and in the immediate post-war years careers officers were in the habit of telling applicants that a B.Sc. (Engineering) was no substitute for practical training.

But the advance of the credentialist system was implacable. The world over, universities took over the responsibility for professional training and in so doing became the main agencies for professional job allocation. Everywhere the belief that people who were credited with having received more 'education' usually earned higher incomes and higher status than those who had less, provided the mainspring for expansionist policies. In the U.K. these policies were a good deal less explosive than in a country hell-bent on rapid modernization like Japan, which had one university in 1890, forty-seven in 1918, 379 in 1969 and 685 in 1976. Nowhere were the effects of credentialism more socially devastating than in the developing countries where the Gadarene rush to secure white-collar occupations inevitably resulted in the hopes and expectations of the great majority being disappointed. The cases of India and Egypt, where masses of unemployable intellectuals had long been a source of social dissidence and political disruption, provided their own early warnings of what was bound to happen in economies whose labour market could not absorb a surplus supply of highly educated people.

In one sense, of course, it is ridiculous to say that anyone can possible be over-educated; in another, it makes perfectly good sense to say that a person can be over-schooled. Just why this is so is argued at length in the present author's book *Education and Schooling*. Dore puts it more succinctly:

> The effect of schooling, the way it alters a man's capacity *and will* to do things, depends not only on what he learns, or the way he learns it, but also on *why* he learns it. That is at the basis of the distinction between schooling which is education, and schooling which is only qualification, a mere process of certificating ... The difference is a difference in what is now fashionably called the 'hidden curriculum'. What the educator is saying implicitly — and sometimes explicitly — to his pupil is: 'learn this or you will not become a good doctor, a skilful carpenter, a fully-developed human being, a good useful citizen; you will not know how to *earn* a living, you will not be able to appreciate the higher pleasures of art or poetry'. What the qualifier says to his pupils is: 'learn this or you will not get the chance to be a doctor or a carpenter; nobody will *give* you a living'. The first appeals to the inner standards of conscience and promises self-achieved fulfilment; the second invokes external arbiters, threatens exclusion, evokes anxiety. The first preserves the teacher:pupil relation as complete in itself; the second makes both dependent on the tyranny of the examiners.[12]

The progressive lengthening of the period spent in formal schooling, now extending into the tertiary stage, has been and remains the subtlest and most powerful of all the pressures behind recent expansionist programmes. From an early age, children have been conditioned to believe that their entire future depends upon paper qualifications they can only obtain through formal schooling. 'Everyone must go to College', 'Education *pays* — stay in school' — these were the kinds of slogan constantly publicized in the U.S.A. where currently more than half the pupils completing high school go on to some kind of full-time course of higher education — and, let it be said, where the educational services have become the largest single employers of labour. In theory, according to some futurologists, *everyone* in a post-industrial society will be profitably engaged in the information business. Which sounds fine. Unfortunately, we live in an imperfect world. Only a decade ago Marjorie Reeves was writing: 'The cat is out of the bag. The simplest equation Education equals Power has suddenly been grasped by the masses the world over. Power to choose your career, power to achieve the standard of living you want, power to exploit the resources of the natural world, power to control and manipulate other people — all these are seen to be conferred by Education'[13].

Tell that to the thousands of college-leavers who today find themselves queuing at the Labour Exchanges. What it amounts to is that the granting of free access to higher education has outrun the actual possibilities for upward social mobility. More simply, the promise of social justice, supposedly inherent in the concept of 'contest mobility', has proved to be delusive, for in encouraging the young to climb higher and higher up the educational ladder of opportunity it has lulled them into imagining not only that there is room at the top but room for nearly everyone. Whereas in 1944 the problem was to convince more pupils that they were capable of getting a degree — and more parents that they could afford to let their children go to university — the problem now is to 'cool out' the masses who take it as a matter of course that higher education owes them a living.

It was no accident, surely, that the publication of Ivan Illich's *Deschooling Society* coincided with the onset of an acute energy crisis. More than anything else, the Opec decision to treble oil prices effectively doused the naive optimism of economists and educationists alike. By 1973 the education industry had become the fastest-growing sector in the economic field. Until then the conviction that all forms of higher education, and certainly university education, were wealth-creating had remained more or less unshakable. An interesting late example of an attempt to validate this was Mark Brownrigg's *Study of the Economic Impact of the University of Stirling*, Scotland's one and only plateglass foundation which opened in 1967[14] (Scotland's other new universities, Heriot-Watt and Strathclyde originated as CATs, while Dundee hived off from St Andrews.) In terms of unit costs per undergraduate Stirling is between four and five times more expensive than the Open University but it was argued, rightly enough, that its effectiveness could not be calculated on so crude and narrow a basis. Brownrigg's analysis, relying on a sophisticated 'regional income multiplier' theorem estimated that the impact of a new university catering for some 1,000 students added about £1 million to local incomes and created between 600 and 800 jobs. Moreover, the university served as a magnet, attracting new industries into the region. According to this, the resulting influx of students, employees and other dependants would exert a substantially beneficial influence on an area of Central Scotland with a population of 100,000. By 1984 (*absit omen!*), if these projections were accurate, the University of Stirling would be primarily responsible for doubling the population and for providing twice as many extra jobs as would otherwise have happened.

As to that, the obvious retort can only be: some hopes! Ten years later it is easier to give credence to veiled hints, some of them dropped in high places, that Stirling is *de trop*, if not totally unnecessary. In the interim the chickens have come home to roost and the powers that be have been forced to recognize the sober truth of Koerner's judgement back in 1966 that 'Some of the distinguishing elements of British universities are expensive enough to make higher education in that country about the most costly in the world at a time when the English economy is weak[15].

That the binary system represented a compromise between the need for preserving 'quality' and the demand for 'quantity', the only possible compromise in the circumstances, is at least arguable. Less convincing, perhaps, is the argument which would have us believe that it has succeeded in getting the best of both worlds. While it is too early to pronounce one way or the other, the record suggests that British policy-making during its formative period has been obsessed with the kind of *idée fixe* which equates higher education with university education and lavishes its favours on the latter as the only imaginable 'centre of excellence'.

Breakthrough in educational technology: the Open University

So far, this account of developments in the expanding and diversifying field of higher education may have given the impression of being more critical and sceptical than appreciative. If so, some *amende honorable* is called for. Happily, the success story of the Open University provides the cue for making it. No other British educational achievement in the post-war era, it is fair to say, has earned the envy and the admiration of the rest of the world as much as this. That its advent was greeted either with apathy or downright hostility on the part of politicians, administrators and academics was all too typical of Britain's inability to spot and back a winner when it saw one. This is not the place to recapitulate its precarious prehistory or to hold up to scorn the forces and factions which would gladly have seen it stifled at birth. Enough to say that since its inception in 1971 the Open University has established itself as an agency for 'distance learning' in the grand manner, with a multi-media instructional system which is second to none, and academic standards which are at least on a par with those of conventional universities.

'Based on an idea of Harold Wilson. Designed by Jennie Lee. Produced and directed by Walter Perry' — these might well be the leading credit titles in a film advertising this radically new departure, an institution of higher learning which goes far to release its students from the age-old constraints of space and time. In fact, the 'idea' first mooted in the Prime Minister's Glasgow speech in 1963 was admittedly inchoate and it was left

to Jennie Lee originally in her capacity as the Minister responsible for the Arts to lick it into shape and supply the passion and
the political muscle needed to overcome opposition from both
sides of the House of Commons and within the D.E.S. From the
outset she was firm in stating the objectives: the O.U. was to
rank as a fully independent university, making no compromise
whatever on standards while at the same time offering access to
all without any entrance qualification.

The choice of name for a university which has no local
habitation and a catchment area covering the whole of the U.K.
was itself significant of the break with the past. By comparison,
all previous universities had been wholly or partially closed
communities. In his 1969 inaugural address as Chancellor, Lord
Crowther affirmed that the O.U. was intended to be open in
four senses — 'as to people', 'as to places', 'as to methods' and,
not least important, 'as to ideas'.

As regards the first of these it was estimated that the pool of
highly motivated adults who would welcome a second chance
would be large enough to ensure that the demand for entry
would not fall for several years. Any estimates had to be based
largely on guesswork. But as Dr Perry explains,

> Many people had, in fact, been born too soon for them to
> benefit from the expansion that followed Robbins. Rough
> calculations indicated that, of the adult population of Britain
> between the ages of 21 and 50, well over a million people fell
> into this category. The Committee was realistic in recognising
> that only a small proportion of this vast group of adults
> would, at a later age, wish to go back into higher education.
> The question at issue was what proportion would be so
> willing. The Committee guessed that 10% might be a
> reasonable figure, and some 100,000 people might therefore
> want to take advantage of the opportunity that the Open
> University would offer.[16]

In the event, the number of students rose from an initial intake
of 19,551 in 1971 to 49,358 in 1975 — and barring quite
disastrous cutbacks in finance, looks like growing continuously
in the future.

Although the original policy of 'first-come-first-served' has had to be somewhat modified (in their own interests some applicants are advised that immediate acceptance is not possible and are placed on the waiting list) the risks taken in adopting it seem to have been justified. O.U. student performance, indeed, has made a mockery of the A-level requirements still insisted upon by other universities as a precondition for entry.

'Open as to places.' To the lighthouse-keeper in a remote island in Shetland as well as to the housewife in her Surbiton home, not to mention the inmates of prison cells, the opportunity for serious study in one's own time and one's own setting without being required to attend at a given centre at given times or to satisfy regulations which stipulate that courses must be completed by a given date, has many advantages. The disadvantages, needless to say, are equally obvious: isolation, the lack of personal contact with tutors and fellow-students, the innumerable distractions which are bound to occur. It has to be conceded that, with the best will in the world, these handicaps are only partly offset by the local and regional study centres and the all-too-short annual summer school which are organized as an integral part of the services provided by the O.U. Well may Dr Perry acknowledge that 'Ours is the most difficult way of getting a degree yet invented by the wit of man'. That the difficulties have been overcome by so many students speaks well for their stamina and is the best proof, if any is needed, that the O.U. offers no soft options.

'Open as to methods'. If the O.U. has succeeded beyond all expectation in establishing itself as a credible and reputable alternative to existing and more costly forms of higher education, it has done so mainly because it has adopted a modern systems approach to the design of its courses and course materials. Other universities have boards of studies: *only the O.U. has course teams*. These teams in which academics, authors, media experts and representatives of the central Institute of Educational Technology join forces in a combined operation, are responsible for defining objectives, tests for their assessment, work assignments, course content and modes of presentation. Far from being a University of the Air — its radio and T.V. programmes account for five to eight per cent of study time at the most — the O.U.'s unique instructional system relies heavily on correspondence material. Each course team plays its part in the preparation, editing, and production of textbooks and readers in what has come to be a large-scale publishing enterprise. If the potential threat to the educational book trade gives rise to disquiet in certain quarters, the sheer quality of Open University Press publications has never been in doubt. So far as value for money is concerned, in nearly every case they represent by far the best buy. Impersonal as self-instruction usually is, one suspects that the O.U. package is at least as effective as the kind of teaching which normally takes place in lecture theatres and seminar groups — at any rate for students who are able and willing to handle it.

In a way, the success of this all-out application of the principles of educational technology is the more surprising in view of the consistent failure of educational technology to live up to the hopes of its early proponents. During the 1960s, first programmed learning and teaching machines, then language laboratories, closed circuit T.V., synchronized slide-tape audio-visual equipment and other mechanical devices had seemed to usher in a 'teaching revolution', only to end by losing what little impact they had. Apart from a recognition of the need for clearly defined objectives and continuous monitoring of these to provide the necessary feedback of information ('immediate knowledge of results') for teacher and pupil alike, by 1970 little or nothing remained of the programmed follow-up projects like computer-assisted instruction, which to many seemed to be throwing good money after bad. The 'white heat' of the technological revolution had turned tepid. Hardware was 'out'. After a decade or more in the ascendant, educational technology, if not entirely discredited, was decidedly under a cloud.

One obvious reason was that it had been adopted piecemeal. Another was that it had relied on mechanical equipment which was as crude as it was limited in usefulness. A third was that it overreached itself in pretending that self-instructional devices could not only supplement but actually supplant the role of teacher. In short, the *disjecta membra* of educational technology existed but ways and means of systematizing them had yet to be found.

The spectacular achievements of the O.U. can to a great extent be attributed to its application of the principles of educational technology in a consistently systematic way. Thus, other universities make extensive use of computers, but only the O.U. is computer-based. Other universities prescribe textbooks and lists for further reading; only the O.U. prepares, edits and publishes its own. Other universities set end-of-term and final examinations, the results of which are announced in due course; only the O.U. provides facilities for continuous assessment and a regular supply of information which enables the student to check his progress.

To say that the O.U. is specifically geared to the provision of mass higher education may seem to vilify it but deserves to be taken as the greatest possible compliment. According to Leslie Wagner, 'The capital cost per student place at the Open University is about 6 per cent of that at conventional universities. And this excludes residential costs. If the latter are included, the Open University's relative cost is about 3 per cent'[17]. Moreover, its teaching costs are not directly related to the number of students, so that the total of 38,424 enrolled in 1973 could easily be doubled without any significant increase in the size of staff. In its long-term planning, the O.U. anticipated reaching a steady state by 1975 with an annual admission rate of 25,000 students and a total student population of 75,000 students. After making allowances for inflation, says Dr Perry, the total annual grant for maintaining the O.U. in this steady state would be £27 million in 1975 values — chicken-feed compared with the sums squandered elsewhere in the name of higher education. Seeing that applications continue to flow in at the rate of 50,000 a year it seems obvious that further economies of scale are possible.

But possibly the O.U.'s most saving grace, and one which other universities might emulate, derives from its built-in procedures for assessment and evaluation. Thanks to these, an experiment which might have gone horribly wrong has turned out better than anyone dared to have hoped.

One other feature of the University in the steady state, on which we would lay great stress, is the achievement of adequate methods of evaluating our courses. The Planning Committee laid great stress on the need for an innovatory institution, embarking on a highly experimental form of teaching, to build in from the beginning ways of estimating how far it had succeeded in meeting the needs of the students … We have tried our best to fulfil these aims and to organise an adequate feedback from the students so that we could gradually improve and refine the whole of our teaching/learning system. The main problem has been to devote enough of our limited funds to the task of analysing and evaluating the programmes we are offering.[18]

Now that the first and second of the objectives laid down in the O.U.'s Royal Charter have been achieved (i.e. 'to provide education of university and professional standards'), it is pertinent to ask what is likely to become of the third — 'to promote the educational wellbeing of the community'. From the beginning it was intended that once the undergraduate programme was completed the next task would be to tackle the urgent problems of retraining, to which end the O.U. has already made a promising start with its post-experience courses. In every walk of life, from medical practitioners to railway signalmen, rapid obsolescence is becoming an occupational hazard which can only be overcome by periodical re-entry into the educational system. 'Refresher courses', 'in-service training', 'recyclage', 'recurrent' education', 'continuing education' — each is indicative of the inadequacy of initial qualifications in a technological society and the pressing need for their updating. From now on, clearly, the responsibility of any institution of higher education, be it university, polytechnic, college of education or whatever, cannot end at graduation. Unfortunately, during a period of financial stringency the neglected field of continuing education is the one which is likely to suffer most severely. Not being labour-intensive, and catering as it does for students who remain in full-time employment anyway, the O.U. is well-placed to give a lead and to act as a catalyst in the emergent field of continuing education.

The O.U. has never lacked critics and detractors. Jealous of it as a parvenu, die-hards are apt to complain that its accomplishments have only been made possibly by its parasitic nature, meaning by that that it relies on the part-time services of academics drawn from other universities, feeding off them like ivy on a tree. More radical critics protest that it is not so innovative as is often claimed, merely another university marketing its wares for a degree-hungry section of the public — as middle-class in its clientele as the rest of them. Walter James, for one, is disposed to regard it as a missed opportunity. As a degree-awarding agency, he agrees, it obviously has a future, at any rate for the underprivileged and dispossessed who are only too eager to pick up the crumbs which fall from the academic community's high table. But even on this reckoning, the fare offered consists (in his own words) of 'plastic packages of soggy bread'[19].

It is true that, so far, the O.U. has done little or nothing to break the monopoly in the credentialist system, i.e. that its main business is transacted via its licence to 'sell' academic awards. Constrained as it is by its charter it is difficult to see how it could have done anything else. This much can be said in its favour, however, that its course offerings are not restricted to its registered students. Just how large its eavesdropping audience is, there is no way of knowing, but as time goes on it may well be that the genuine success of the O.U. will be measured not so much in terms of the number of its graduates as by the size of its non-registered members, the ones who are able and willing to avail themselves of some form of 'higher learning', provided that they can take it or leave it and without coveting a piece of parchment by way of reward.

All this may seem to imply a disinterested approach to learning which is exceptional rather than the rule. On the face of things, certainly, the motive power behind the drive for recurrent education stems from vocational self-interest. Dumazedier's vision of a life-cycle in which leisure, not work, will be the dominant element and in which cultural pursuits will take precedence over the skills involved in earning a living, cannot fail to seem utopian. In the present economic recession the prospects for a 'learning society' of the kind envisaged by Husén and Plan Europe 2000 are bound to appear too dim to be worth contemplating.

At the same time there remains a vast area of unaccredited learning, the kind which has its locus not in any formal institution but in the family, the peer group, at the work-place, in the mass media, above all in the numberless voluntary associations which proliferate in contemporary society. It is to these, rather than to the limited sectors occupied by formal higher education, that the attention of those who are concerned to translate the rhetoric of continuous education into practical reality is now turning. In a changing world, the universities continue to play an active part in what used to be called the 'extension movement': witness, for example, the fact that the University of Glasgow accommodates some 10,000 students enrolled for degree courses during the daytime, and rather more adults following cultural and recreational evening courses organized by an Extra-Mural Department serving the west of Scotland.

As yet, the practical implications of the theory of continuous education (a term more appropriate in English usage than 'permanent education' and one which embraces 'further', 'higher', 'adult', 'recurrent' and 'continuing' education as well as pre-school learning) are more revolutionary than is commonly supposed. To quote Dr Perry again:

> Once continuing education is available, the whole question of radical changes in the pattern of initial education can be re-opened. For one has then decided which is the horse and which the cart. Then, and only then, could we approach the ultimate goal: a system of higher education which would provide for the needs of all, the scholar and the practical man, the excellent and the able, the school-leaver and the adult, without the risk that providing for the one will prejudice the best provision of the other.[20]

The way ahead

Beyond saying that the provision of British higher education is vastly more extensive and its pattern more varied than it was in 1944 there seems little point in trying to draw up a balance sheet of the profits accruing from, and the losses incurred in, the developments which have since taken place. If Sir Mark Smith is right, the outcome is a serious imbalance — no lack of graduates but not enough of the kind needed to satisfy the nation's industrial needs. In an age of cultural flux, and in the absence of any semblance of manpower-planning involving the direction of labour, it is easy to see why we are left with a dozen or more sociologists for every engineer. All along, the assumption has been that the service sector was itself wealth-creating and could therefore be expanded more or less indefinitely. It now appears that the 'information business', like any other, is not exempt from bankruptcy and that many of those engaged in it turn out to be caterpillars of the commonwealth, battening on the reduced sector responsible for basic production. To put it another way, some aspects of British higher education invite the charge of being work-shy!

As with allegations of falling standards in the schools, the charge is easy to make and extraordinarily difficult to prove. That it is not entirely without substance may be inferred from the fact, now that belt-tightening is the order of the day, that most universities find it far from impossible to carry the same work-load as before with reduced resources — though none is willing to admit it. Postgraduate programmes are to be drastically curtailed and fees for them trebled. Many colleges of education are to be closed down. In the realignments which must follow, major changes in the distribution of resources are going to be needed if the present wastage caused by duplication and multiplication of effort is to be corrected. Maybe it is too late for a rationalization of the crazy-paving pattern of higher education in Britain to be practical politics — and maybe it is not even desirable. In the struggle for survival the chances are that a principle of natural selection will operate, with the older and bigger fish swallowing the small fry. Nonetheless, it is a fair guess that the eventual shape of the tertiary stage will be decided by developments in 'open' institutions which do not answer to the university stereotype.

References

1 T. Burgess (ed.), *The Shape of Higher Education* (Corn-market 1972), p.16.
2 M. Beloff, *The Plateglass Universities* (Secker, 1968), p.181.
3 Robbins Report, *Higher Education* (H.M.S.O., 1963), para. 784.
4 ibid., para. 630.
5 ibid., paras. 621, 630.
6 ibid., Appendix One, p.79.
7 M. Trow, 'Binary dilemmas: an American view', in Tyrrell Burgess (ed.), *The Shape of Higher Education* (Cormarket, 1972), pp.24-5.
8 G. Fowler, 'DES Ministers and the curriculum', in Alan Harris *et al.*, *Curriculum Innovation* (Open University Press, 1975), pp.62-3.
9 A. Briggs, 'Developments in higher education in the United Kingdom', in W.R. Niblett (ed.), *Higher Education: Demand and Response* (Tavistock, 1969), p.106.
10 J.D. Koerner, *Reform in Education* (Weidenfeld, 1968), p.217.
11 R. Dore, *The Diploma Disease* (Allen & Unwin, 1976), pp.4-5.
12 ibid., pp.8-9.
13 M. Reeves, *Eighteen Plus* (Routledge, 1970), p.11.
14 M. Brownrigg, *A Study of the Economic Impact of the University of Stirling* (Scottish Academic Press, 1974).
15 Koerner, op. cit., p.228.
16 W. Perry, *The Open University* (Open University Press, 1976), p.135.
17 L. Wagner, 'The economic implications', in J. Tunstall (ed.), *The Open University Opens* (Routledge, 1974), p. 21.
18 Perry, op. cit., p.260.
19 W. James 'The future of the Open University', paper presented at the Agnelli Symposium, Turin, 1973.
20 Perry, op. cit., p.285.

5 The control of education

Ministers and Secretaries of State for Education and Science come and go — sixteen of them at the latest count, most of them leaving little or no trace of their brief tenure of office — but the permanent secretariat not only goes on for ever but continues to grow more powerful. This increase in bureaucratic control is a worldwide phenomenon by no means peculiar to Britain or to the educational services in which, nevertheless, it rightly causes disquiet. According to Torsten Husén, during the past twenty years the number of educational administrators in all the industrialized countries has increased twice as rapidly as the number of students and teachers, with the result that we now have a separate managerial class which acts as a kind of Praetorian Guard, an army of officials who have a vested interest in the running of the educational mega-machine and in its maintenance. During the period under review both primary and secondary schools, especially the latter, have become progressively larger, as has the unit of local administration.

The expansion of the education system also extends to its organisational machinery [says Husén]. Education takes place within the framework of increasingly larger administrative units, often created under the illusory belief in economy of size. The hierarchy of decision-makers has grown higher and higher with the convergence of more and more power to the summit and the proliferation of time-consuming channels for the transaction of business. In spite of assurances to the contrary in an era when 'participation' and 'grassroot involvement' are 'in' words, increased centralisation is a fact, if we bear in mind that it can also apply to the local school administration. As more links are inserted in the hierarchical chain and the direct contacts between decision-makers and the classrooms diminish, formalism becomes magnified and attention is diverted from the substance of education. Traditional models of bureaucratic administration in education have recently been brought into question. The crucial problem is to what extent bureaucratic steering is compatible with the educative functions which the schools and the teachers are supposed to fulfill.[1]

In law, the Secretary of State is charged with powers of promotion and direction which are limited only by the proviso that he is accountable for them to the House of Commons and must not act unreasonably. For the architects of the 1944 Act these were thought to be adequate safeguards; today, when law and order are, to put it gently, less firmly established, any ruling of the highest courts in the land concerning ministers who are alleged to have exceeded their powers is liable to be disputed.

In practice, of course, a strong-minded minister can impose his will on the officials responsible for the running of his department, but more often than not it appears that he has no option but to follow their expert advice and to that extent is in their hands. This is not to say that the Secretary of State is a figurehead, though the description certainly fits some of those who have held this office, rather that any effective power he has needs to be exercised indirectly and then only after consultations with his colleagues in the Cabinet and with a host of other bodies. In the meantime the regular business of the D.E.S. is conducted behind the scenes, assiduously screened from public scrutiny. The worrying thing is that D.E.S. officialdom is not accountable to anyone except the Secretary of State himself, so that when, as has happened more than once, the advice it offers turns out to be disastrously wrong it is usually too late to correct the error for the simple reason that by the time it is discovered a new Secretary of State has taken charge of the Department. Thus, despite her reputation for being strong-minded, Mrs Thatcher's 1972 White Paper, *A Framework for Expansion*, could hardly have been wider of the mark than it was, thanks to being based on the number of births between 1968 and 1970 when, it is claimed, there was no clear indication that the birth rate was falling. In other walks of life a miscalculation of this magnitude would have justified the severest censure on those responsible for it, if not their dismissal for gross incompetence. To excuse it on the grounds that 'D.E.S. statistical projections are always behind the times whatever government is in power', is really quite nonsensical[2].

Behind this cloak of secrecy 'the note of authority at the centre', which Lester Smith was the first to detect and criticize in the 1944 Act, has gradually been accentuated although it has consistently been played down. Time and again, ministers have disclaimed any intention or wish to exercise their powers of direction. Without questioning their sincerity, nevertheless the trend towards central control cannot be disguised. The spirit which allowed George Tomlinson to declare that 'Minister knows nowt about curriculum', is today as dead as the spirit of Dunkirk.

Similarly, the relationship between central and local government, formerly one of a partnership between equals, has become much more one-sided. One result of the exponential growth of educational expenditure has been to strengthen the hand of the central government, which alone can provide the vast sums of money needed to maintain all the services of the state system and which has its own ways and means of deciding how that money is distributed and how it is spent. To trace the various strategies designed to secure firmer financial control at the centre would require full-length treatment in a separate review of developments since 1944: enough, here, to remark that no one doubts that the control *is* firmer. As with the curriculum it is disguised in subtle ways. A typical example, which caused a furore at the time, was the government's decision in 1959 to introduce a system of block grants in place of the largely percentage formula which had obtained since 1944. Ostensibly, the argument was that a block grant was in the interests of local autonomy, allowing L.E.A.s to spend as much or as little as they thought fit on the educational services — and that it would reduce administrative costs. Critics of the new scheme objected, not without good cause, that it could be interpreted as an ingenious device for slowing down expansion since any additional expenditure would henceforth fall on the rates — and local councillors were (and are) notorious for being more interested in keeping down the rates than in anything else. John Vaizey's verdict on this issue which, like so many others, now seems to have been a storm in a teacup, seems as valid today as it was at the time:

> Since the expansion of education is agreed to be of great importance at present, and should not be subject to undue financial restraint, it is difficult to see the argument for introducing a block grant system at the present time. There is a great deal to be said, indeed, for the opposite — for increasing the rate of grant paid from central funds on most educational expenditure. On the other hand, the issue of the method of grant payment is not as serious as the controversy might suggest since so many outgoings are in fact fixed.[3]

What cannot escape notice, however, is that major issues of this kind are decided over the heads of the mass of people whose lives are affected by them and who are virtually excluded from the decision-making process because they do not have access to the information needed to form and express an opinion on such issues. As regards the introduction of a block grant, for example, it is doubtful whether more than a handful of directors of education really understood the pros and cons or the long-term implications, certain that most teachers did not, and equally certain that laymen, for their part, were so completely in the dark as to be totally uninterested.

Following the 1972 Redcliffe-Maud regional reorganization of local government in England and Wales and the 1973 Wheatley reorganization in Scotland, this distancing of officialdom from the electorate has been further increased. Unlike in the U.S.A., where educational administration is kept apart from the other public services so that 'we the people' are free to elect their own school board representatives, it has never been possible for British electors to have any say in the choice of members of their local education committee. This is only one of a number of reasons why the percentage voting in local government elections in Britain is much lower than in any other European country; and while it is arguable that there is still plenty of scope for low-level decision-making in local affairs — in town, district and parish councils, for instance, and in the innumerable voluntary common-interest groups and associations which flourish as never before in contemporary British society, the fact remains that the concentration of power is located in the uppermost echelons of a bureaucracy — the new ruling class.

Under the old dispensation it was at least possible for the man in the street to know the name of his local director of education, if only as a rubber-stamped signature on a letter from County Hall, even possible to know the names of some members of the education committee. Under the new order, even this tenuous connection is likely to be severed. A mammoth regional authority like Strathclyde comprising half the population of Scotland and responsible not only for the affairs of a vast industrial conurbation but for sparsely populated rural areas which are geographically and culturally remote from its Glasgow head-quarters, is a power complex in its own right with tier upon tier of committees and sub-committees whose deliberations, how-ever faithfully reported in the press, are so far removed from the public as to seem none of that public's concern. The issue of news-sheets announcing plans for developments in the various districts of the region and the setting-up of locally elected School Councils (with limited responsibilities defined by the regional authority to ensure their impotence) are poor substitutes for the kind of participatory democracy which is needed.

Unlike the situation in England, where the creation of fewer and larger L.E.A.s may be seen as a means of facilitating more central control, reorganization north of the border looks like having the opposite effect. Hitherto the Scottish tradition in education has always been more authoritarian than in England, local administrators and teachers alike more or less toeing the line laid down in St Andrews House without demur. Today, some of the larger regional authorities are in a position to challenge the Secretary of State for Scotland himself: indeed, the chairman of Midlothian Region has recently ventured the opinion that the Scottish Education Department is now redundant and that many of its functions, including the inspection of schools, can be taken over and discharged more efficiently by the regions. This underlines Husén's point about the effects of centralization in stifling grassroots participation at the local level being no less serious than those experienced as a result of central governmental action: St Andrews House or Midlothian Regional Authority, D.E.S. or Inner London, either way the effects are everywhere the same.

Must all this be seen as a last-ditch effort to shore up the ruins of an outmoded and discredited system? It begins to look that way. As things are, certainly, it is difficult to see what form a new Education Act might take or, indeed, what useful purpose it would serve. To be sure, there is plenty of tidying up to be done, notably as regards the Middle School's straddling the conventional age of transfer from the primary to the secondary stage, and plenty of unfinished business at the pre-school stage. While there can be no question of a further raising of the school-leaving age, there remains a whole set of problems arising in the upper secondary school, many of them chronic, for which solutions must be found sooner rather than later; not to mention the inchoate state of affairs in the emergent tertiary sector. But the reformist zeal and the political will which inspired the 1944 concordat are now so completely lacking that anything more than a consolidating Act seems out of the question — as does the prospect of reviving the Christian principles embodied in the 1944 legislation.

What the new Act might well do, of course, would be to make explicit the concept of continuous education implicit in the 'three progressive stages' envisaged in 1944, in other words to draw up a charter for lifelong learning. To do this, unfortunately, would require revolutionary changes in the existing system and no less revolutionary changes in the scope and meaning of the educational process as a whole. This is what the authors of the Faure Commission report, *Learning To Be*, significantly a document which aroused little interest in Britain, had in mind when they asserted that any meaningful reform of the established system of education must involve 'the indispensable remoulding of all its elements — theory and practice, structure and methods, management and organization'. This is a tall order, many would say a utopian day-dream, and in its present mood and condition the country is clearly unprepared to commit itself to anything like so radical a course.

The trouble is that in our over-schooled society education has come to serve as a secular substitute for religion and that the faith which it once inspired, and still inspires in the uninitiated, has now given way to profound scepticism. Education, in the restricted sense of formal schooling (in effect, the only sense in which the term is generally understood), has failed to live up to its promises, or so it seems. In the first place, it has disappointed the hopes of those who saw it as the means of achieving equality of opportunity, an ideal which recedes before every advance in the rainbow quest for it. In the second, it has not produced the economic returns expected from it. As a guarantee for improved social status and lucrative life-earnings it still has its uses, but as the 'diploma disease' worsens, even this guarantee is certain to be jeopardized. Again, the provision of mass schooling may be credited with raising standards of living, but it is by no means evident that there has been any comparable improvement in the quality of life (admittedly a hazy concept, hazier than that concerning falling standards in scholastic attainment or in public morality, but the very fact that it causes concern is suggestive). While it would be defeatist to concede that, when all is said and done, 'more' *has* meant 'worse' the evidence of discontent and apathy among the ranks of teenagers who are compelled to endure an extended school-life highlights the fallacy of supposing that education is something that everyone wants. If education is to be equated with institutional schooling, then it is only too apparent that many have had as much of it as they can stand. Anyone who doubts this should observe the riotous scenes on the terraces when the young monsters who support Chelsea, Manchester United and other football clubs run berserk. Make no mistake about it, these are the products of a school system which stands indicted on the charge of cultivating anti-social attitudes and, which is worse, a positive hatred of learning in any shape or form.

It may be thought that this is pitching it too strongly. Is it not premature to infer that we are witnessing the demise of an outmoded system, and wholly irresponsible to describe that system as discredited? Despite the shrill prophecies of the deschoolers, the mega-machine shows no signs of grinding to a halt: on the contrary, the tight control over it by politicians, administrators, teachers (yes, teachers, too) and all those dedicated to the task of system maintenance not only ensures that it is kept in smooth running order but also that it continues to expand its field of operation. Like a giant industrial plant engaged in the people-processing business, the statutory system of education is an integral part of the welfare state, too big to be easily dismantled yet at the same time in need of retooling and in even greater need of scrapping some of its erstwhile priorities and diversifying its products.

So long as institutional schooling was the be-all and end-all, central control over the education system could be seen as a menace. In an educative society which is information-rich and whose members are capable of learning as and when they wish, the possibility of such control ceases to exist. But for the fact that too many people's zest for learning is impaired in early youth, brain-damaged, so to speak, by the experience of schooling, it might be said that we already live in an educative society. The existing system *is* outmoded in the sense that our educational institutions are still based on nineteenth-century models, i.e. as filling stations to which the young are expected to come and get their supply of knowledge and skills to serve them for the rest of their lives. In a word, the entire emphasis has been on initial education. In the days when knowledge was in relatively short supply, formal instruction in the classroom was, and to some extent still is, a convenient and efficient delivery system for initial education, but with the 'knowledge explosion' to contend with and the rapid obsolescence of knowledge and basic skills it has proved to be increasingly difficult, not to say downright impossible, to pack even the essentials of general education into nine, ten or eleven years of school attendance. Because time was so short and because teachers and pupils alike were under pressure on the understanding that it was a case of now or never — no second chance for those who missed out or dropped out — initial education assumed an exaggerated importance. Learning itself came to be associated more or less exclusively with one kind of cognitive skill — scholastic learning — always *in statu pupillari* and usually as the result of formal instruction. In the process the impression that no significant learning could take place in the absence of a teacher was studiously fostered, as was the no less false idea that the job of teaching was the monopoly of a professional class of men and women who had been specially trained for it. Strange, this, seeing that everyone knows that there are whole realms of learning not dealt with in any school curriculum, and that in society at large all kinds of people — parents, parsons, lovers, journalists, media men, musicians, artists, to name but a few in an endless list — are constantly engaged, albeit informally, in teaching. Strange, possibly, but the myth persists.

> The whole administrative hierarchy of education, as it grew up, followed the model of industrial bureaucracy [says Alvin Toffler]. The very organization of knowledge into permanent disciplines was grounded on industrial assumptions. Children marched from place to place and sat in assigned stations. Bells rang to announce changes of time. The inner life of the school thus became an anticipatory mirror, a perfect introduction to industrial society. The most criticized features of education today — the regimentation, lack of individualization, the rigid systems of seating, grouping, grading and marking, the authoritarian role of the teacher — are precisely those that made mass public education so effective an instrument of adaptation for its place and time.[4]

Reluctant as the authorities are to face up to the fact that the kind of initial education which proved effective enough in the past must today be considered inappropriate and largely misapplied, they can hardly fail to be daunted by its prohibitive costs. Resources being limited, we simply cannot afford to entertain the illusion that formal schooling is all-important and that, of necessity, it must be completed within a given time span. From now on learning throughout the period of adult life is going to be a necessity rather than a luxury indulged in by a dilettante minority. Already, doctors, teachers and other professional workers in the U.S.A. are required to take further training every five or six years (every three years for G.P.s in two states) or face the prospect of being declared redundant, and as time goes on this is certain to become common practice in most occupations. As yet, legislation designed to meet the needs of workers for recurrent education, in-service training as it used to be called, has scarcely been mooted in Britain which, in this respect at least, lags sadly behind France, Sweden and other European nations.

And if, as we are assured is going to happen in the future, it is going to be necessary for a person to switch jobs twice or thrice in the course of a working career, to adapt himself to constantly changing circumstances and requirements, to acquire new skills, learning afresh as he goes and unlearning old habits and ways of thinking, how absolutely vital it is going to be to revise our ideas about the aims, content and methods of basic schooling. Easy to talk about 'education in the future tense', trite but true to say that children should be taught to learn how to learn, though not very helpful seeing that in practice no one really knows how it can be done, least of all specialist subject teachers.

At this point [argues Henri Janne] a closer examination of the educational implications of the frequent and often profound technological changes characteristic of industrial societies seems necessary. Jobs, whether skilled or unskilled, are already requiring re-adaptation or will be totally changed in their knowledge and skill components, and this trend will accelerate. Old trades and specialities are disappearing while new specialized jobs have to be filled. This means that training must become a fundamental factor of work organization and study a recurrent activity of a large number of workers. Therefore, school education cannot continue to supply youth with clearly defined knowledge, very specialized competences or skills *relating to definite types of work*. The 'encyclopedic' character of traditional schooling beyond the level of general elementary education ... must be replaced by wide and versatile but in-depth education in the mastery of certain types of 'logic' and languages constituting a sufficiently homogeneous epistemological approach to a given field: mathematics, a sector of technology and its scientific bases, communication, languages, history and culture, etc. That kind of education should aim not so much at acquisition of knowledge and information as rather at intellectual ability and practice in solving new problems in a given sector.[5]

Sage advice for those seeking to define the essentials of a common-core curriculum, no doubt, but somewhat vague, as are the Council of Europe's recommendations:

The schooling of youth will be less and less a matter of acquiring knowledge (soon outdated) and information (provided more comprehensively elsewhere) but will be more and more devoted to the acquisition of methods of thought, adaptive attitudes, critical reactions and disciplines which teach how to learn. It should also foster the expectation of education to come, convey familiarity with the means of recourse to it and enable pupils and students to find methods of learning which suit them best. It will be impossible to teach the requisite flexibility of reaction except through appropriate activities entailing participation and responsibility. The schooling period will become more active and involve personal responsibility and leisure time for the absorption of culture. (The traditional status of young people at school prolongs their infantile state.)[6]

The best hope, surely, lies in the resourcefulness of the children themselves: in general, they are a good deal more adaptable than their elders and mentors and, given the facilities and a modicum of priming, are quite capable of learning for and by themselves. Born curious, as R.A. Hodgkin's book title aptly puts it, they need to be preserved in this blessed state at all costs. If there is one overriding objective in initial education it is precisely this: that at the very least pupils leave school with a genuine liking for learning, eager and able to pursue it in the wider world. To repeat, this is the one objective which formal schooling far too often fails to achieve.

To ask a person, 'When did you stop learning?', is as ridiculous as to ask him when he stopped breathing. To most educationists, though not to anthropoligists, the notion that learning is as natural as breathing seems almost quixotic. Only latterly have they been forced to recognize what anthropologists have always known, i.e. that education and learning are far from being coterminous with schooling, and that every individual learns about others and about his environments as he progresses through his own life-cycle regardless of whether schools exist or not. The dimensions of learning transcend those encompassed within even the most humane and distinguished academic circles. Babes in arms learn from their mothers, lovers learn from each other, children from their parents (and vice versa), youths from their peer group, from the neighbourhood, above all from the mass media. The locus of learning varies from hour to hour and from day to day, now at the breakfast table, now at the workbench, now at a meeting of shop stewards, now in the pub, now listening to the news, now digging the garden, now browsing over some travel brochures with a mind to the summer holidays.

All of which sounds dangerously like the easy-going aphorism which assures us that we live and learn, and dangerously like the advocacy which led to the trivialization of so-called 'Life Adjustment' courses in the U.S.A. twenty-odd years ago. The point is that modern man is in the unprecedented situation of having at his disposal resources for learning so infinitely rich and varied that he risks being overwhelmed by them. An information-rich society is not necessarily an educative or a learning society unless its members can make systematic, selective and critical use of

the resources available to them. We know what happens otherwise: 'Information inundates the minds instead of provoking
their structuralisation; the results being "mosaic culture" and
world-wide cultural tribalism'[7].

As 1984 draws nearer, then, it is no accident that eminent
forward-thinkers nowadays are losing interest in the narrow
sector occupied by the learner's schooldays and focussing their
attention on the prospects and problems arising in the field of
lifelong learning. Possibly because we in Britain like to think of
ourselves as pragmatic and empirical, the kind of people who
prefer to get on with the job rather than indulge in high-flown
rhetoric, relatively little interest or enthusiasm has been displayed so far for the kind of plans for permanent education
currently being formulated by other E.E.C. member nations or
by international agencies such as UNESCO, O.E.C.D. and the
Council of Europe. For one thing, we do not take kindly to the
term 'permanent' education — in English usage it sounds awkward and pretentious, besides smacking of translation from the
French. For another, we find the literature in this field of
discourse so turgid as to be decidedly off-putting, its arguments
too spiced with wishful thinking as to be less than convincing.
Worst of all, even if we settle for calling it continuous education
(not to be confused with continuing education which represents
only one part of it), we are unsure what it means in practice. Let
it be said right away that the whole idea of continuous education
is unlikely to command or deserve popular support so long as it
tends to be associated with the notion of lifelong schooling —
more nursery classes for 2-3-year-olds, more in-service training
for workers, more courses for geriatrics — in short, as Henri
Janne says, 'a nightmare worthy of Kafka'.

What, then, is implied by the concept of continuous education? Bertrand Schwartz, one of the founding fathers of '*l'éduca-
tion permanente*' and director of the Plan Europe 2000 project
explains it as follows:

Permanent education is not so much a new set of aims for
education as an overall design (and in this sense fairly recent)
for strategies to be implemented in achieving these aims. We

define it here as a process of integrating all phases of education in a true space-time continuum, by implementing a range of means (institutional, material, human) which make this integration possible. Although a recent idea, it may also be regarded as transient, because one can imagine that by the year 2000, or even before, the idea that education is permanent will have become such normal practice that it will be referred to simply as education, its being understood that education means permanent education. In the context of permanent education the term implies the clear statement of the faults and malfunctions of present systems and their causes, with the purpose of convincing and mobilising opinion so that things can be changed. It is a political tool which will allow us to choose today what we wish our future to be tomorros.[8]

Less futurological was Paul Lengrand's answer when I put it too him that those of us who championed the cause of lifelong education were duty-bound to explain our reasons for doing so in language that was readily intelligible to laymen:

By lifelong education we mean quite simply that education is not restricted to schooling. On the contrary, its influence extends over all the sectors of the learner's existence, private as well as public — his family and professional relationships, his politics, his social activities, his leisure pursuits and so on. It makes its appeal to all kinds of agencies: school, college and university but equally the family, the community and the world of work, books, press, theatre and the media for mass communication. What it amounts to is that the educational enterprise is a global and continuous process which takes place from the moment of birth to the death of the individual: a process which implies in a circular relationship the education of children, adolescents and adults at different ages and stages of development. If education is to become permanent and all-embracing it follows that its content, its methods and the training of the specialised personnel in the various sectors of the educational enterprise must be very radically changed.[9]

Michael Huberman, Piaget's successor as co-Director of the Faculty of Psychology and Educational Sciences at the University of Geneva and author of the 1973 UNESCO report, *Understanding Change in Education*, was even more forthright in expressing his views on the subject:

> I think that the whole issue is very badly defined. It has become the province of philosophers and politicians who have confused it beyond recognition. Let me put it this way: 'permanent education' means very simply, solving the problems one faces in one's life. Whenever I arrange a trip, when I try to get a new job, or when I try to stop someone blocking the view from my window with a skyscraper, I am engaged in 'permanent education'. For some of these problems I need to use resources other than myself. I may need other people, or books, or I may need instruments. I may even need an institution (e.g. to follow a course of study) although this is rare. The key question is: do I have access to the people, information and instruments which I need in order to solve my problems? Getting more of *that* is what the extension of 'permanent education' is all about. It is not about adding on courses and institutions for adults.[10]

Monsieur Jourdain, it will be recalled, was delighted and surprised to discover that he had been talking prose all his life. By the same token, it seems that we are at last becoming conscious that continuous education is a present reality, not a figment of the planners' imagination. This England of ours is full of it. If we care to look around we can find it in action wherever we go, most of it happily *not* under the control of the D.E.S.! Spontaneous, unsponsored, unsupervised, it tends to go unnoticed, dispersed as it is throughout the length and breadth of society. We can see its outward and visible signs in some of the new emergent institutions — the Open University, the multi-purpose schools, community centres, festivals of all kinds, resource centres, local T.V. installations and the rest — but not the inward urge impelling ordinary people to seek self-knowledge and to lead a fuller life. '*Plus est en vous*' might well be their motto, the conviction that each and every individual has within him the latent power for continuous personal growth. To date, the effects of mass education have been to condition people in the belief that they can never become anything better than they are and that there is no point in their trying. The consequences are only too apparent in the mindless behaviour of large sections of contemporary society, old folk who are tired and bewildered, young folk who are seemingly adrift. As things are, it has to be confessed, lifelong learning assumes some uncanny forms — weird cults, quasi-religious sects, protest movements and whatever turns their adherents on. Much of it is superficial, ephemeral and irresponsibly escapist, some of it depraved to the point of being unmentionable. Not surprising this, seeing that the problem of finding a pattern that 'makes sense' out of a mosaic culture is difficult enough even for those who do have access to the necessary people, information and instruments. Only when all, and not a favoured few, can work out their own solution and salvation will Britain once again become a land of hope and maybe not without glory.

References

1 T. Husén, discussion paper presented at the Aspen Institute seminar on 'The Future of Institutional Schooling', Berlin, September 1976.
2 N. St John Stevas, letter in *Daily Telegraph*, 22 April 1977.
3 J. Vaizey, *The Control of Education* (Faber, 1963), pp.155-6.
4 A. Toffler, *Future Shock*, 5th edn. (Pan Books, 1973), p.362.
5 H. Janne, 'Theoretical foundation of lifelong education: a sociological perspective', in R.H. Dave (ed.), *Foundations of Lifelong Education* (Pergamon for UNESCO Institute of Education, 1976), pp.152-3.
6 *Permanent Education: the Basis and Essentials* (Council for Cultural Cooperation, Council of Europe, 1973), p.22.
7 ibid., p.3.
8 B. Schwartz, in G. Fragnière (ed.), *Education Without Frontiers* (Duckworth, 1976), pp.54-5.

9 W.K. Richmond, 'The future of education: a dialogue with Paul Lengrand', *Scottish Educational Journal*, December 1976.

10 W.K. Richmond, *After Piaget: a Dialogue with Michael Huberman* (in press).

Index